Agile Management

Agile Management

The Fast and Flexible Approach to Continuous Improvement and Innovation in Organizations

Mike Hoogveld

BEP BUSINESS EXPERT PRESS

Agile Management: The Fast and Flexible Approach to Continuous Improvement and Innovation in Organizations
Copyright © Business Expert Press, LLC, 2018.

First published in 2018 by
Business Expert Press, LLC
222 East 46th Street, New York, NY 10017
www.businessexpertpress.com

ISBN-13: 978-1-94744-183-5 (paperback)
ISBN-13: 978-1-94744-184-2 (e-book)

Business Expert Press Portfolio and Project Management Collection

Collection ISSN: 2156-8189 (print)
Collection ISSN: 2156-8200 (electronic)

Cover and interior design by S4Carlisle Publishing Services
Private Ltd., Chennai, India

First edition: 2018

10 9 8 7 6 5 4 3 2 1

Printed in the United States of America.

Dedication

For Suzanne, Julius, and Floris

Abstract

An environment that is changing ever faster and deeper; markets that are becoming more dynamic and complex; competitor and customer behavior that is increasingly unpredictable—these developments are affecting all organizations. Whoever wants to survive in the future needs to adapt with lightning speed. Increasing numbers of organizations recognize that traditional ways of working are no longer adequate. They lack agility.

In this book, agility expert Mike Hoogveld shows us what we can learn from smart start-ups and other successful, innovative organizations. Using many academic insights and practical examples, he describes how to make your organization responsive by focusing on continuous improvement. Thus, he gives a very concrete answer to the crucial question with which so many organizations are struggling: How do we increase our agility?

The book includes an agile assessment to determine the agility of your organization. The book remains number-one bestseller in the Netherlands.

Keywords

Agile, change, customer centricity, high performance, innovation, leadership, lean, management, marketing, scrum, startup, team

Contents

Preface

I am, to be precise, 1 meter and 94 centimeters tall. And I weigh 93 kilos.

Quite a confession with which to start a book . . . But it's not my goal to confess to you something about my physical fitness. Or to see how quickly you can calculate my BMI (24.7). So, you might ask, why do I share this with you.

To give a little air to one of my small frustrations. And this is not about a too-short bed in a holiday cottage, impossible postures in an airplane seat, or the fact that there are still very few beautiful clothes available in my size. What then?

It has to do with sport. For example, squash, which I find immensely enjoyable—not to watch but to play. Only, I'm not so good at it, and that makes it a lot less fun. Losing all the time gets boring after a while. That's why I stopped. Was it my technique? Tactical insight? Fitness? Sadly not. To put it clinically, it had everything to do with the inertia of mass.

For some reason, it seemed that all my opponents had the opposite physique to me. If we use a boxing analogy, they were clearly more "super flyweight" and I was more "heavyweight." And that led to a pretty unequal struggle because strength is not so important in squash. It is mainly about tactics, technique, and mobility. With regard to tactics and technique, my opponents were not really superior to me, but in mobility . . . enough said. Because of their smaller bodies and lower weight, they were simply much faster and more agile. Their nimble turning and sprinting meant they responded much easier and faster to unexpected shots. They adapted directly to my strokes while I crashed into the walls feeling like a hippopotamus or simply fell over. After a while, in addition to a bad mood, I also developed chronic pain in my lower back.

I experience something similar in other sports. If I join my talented son in a game of father–son football, I clearly don't look like Messi, to put it mildly. And along the rugged mountain-bike trail here in the dunes, I am always overtaken by men with small, light bodies. I thought maybe boxing would suit me, but my opponents seemed to be faster than their shadows; often I felt like the punch bag.

Initially, I thought it was me: I was just too slow. But friends with similar physiques to mine seem to have exactly the same exasperation. They also avoid sports that require agility, maneuverability, and quick adjustments. Like them, I focus now on sports in which these factors play a negligible role, such as golf, rowing, swimming, running, and cycling—sports with predictable movements. And I stick with those (sports such as bowling, curling, and darts I leave to others, no matter how beautiful the shirts they wear).

What struck me about the sports that are better suited for my physique is that smaller, lighter men often are incredibly good at these too. And, naturally, that got me thinking: it seems like properties such as speed, agility, and maneuverability make the difference in sports characterized by frequent dynamic movements. That triggered my curiosity in my work as a consultant and in my PhD research. Could it be that the qualities of speed, agility, and maneuverability might also be important for organizations? So that organizations operating in dynamic environments, that have these characteristics, are more successful than organizations that lack them, or have them to a lesser extent?

So, a decade or so ago, I came across the path of *agility* and dived deeply and completely into it. There was a kind of snowball effect. While reading and interviewing, I was inspired by Darwin's discoveries, by Juran's rediscovery of Pareto's *80/20 rule,* and by Deming's *Plan–Do–Check–Act* approach to continuous improvement. By Toyota's success and Boyd's *OODA cycle.* By the possibilities *Scrum* offers and the incredible results achieved in English cycling. And in recent years, also, by the Lean Start-up methodology. Fantastic; a whole new world opened up for me.

What immediately struck me in my consulting practice was that very few organizations are really agile. Most were able to adjust to competitor or customer changes in the market, but only very slowly, while they just complained that change kept happening and that it kept happening faster and faster. They lacked adaptability and, moreover, they were totally unaware of the phenomenon of *agility.*

Therefore, I decided to translate my insights into a process suited to those organizations, by combining proven methodologies and, where necessary, supplementing them with my own solutions. Through experimentation, I finely honed the concepts into an "agile management" approach which, in principle, can be applied to almost any organization.

The insights I gained during my fascinating journey, I would like to share with you, in the form of this book. It combines theoretical knowledge with a practical approach and practical tools. I hope this can inspire you as I too was inspired by the many books, articles, videos, studies, lectures, conversations, projects, and case studies that I have used.

I wish you lots of fun and success with your own agile voyage of discovery!

Mike Hoogveld
Bergen, September 2017

CHAPTER 1

Introduction

Good is the enemy of great.
—Jim Collins

This chapter helps you to get a grip on the contents of this book. It provides you with an introduction to the phenomenon of agility and makes it clear why this is relevant to your organization. It tells you what agile management is and is not, and what kind of problems agile management can solve for you. Furthermore, it offers you a brief overview of the content of the following chapters, so that you can navigate quickly and easily through the book.

1.1 The Organization as a Top Athlete

If you look at professional sports, what do you think is the difference between a rower and a wild-water kayaker? Between a speed skater and an ice-hockey player? A road-cyclist and a mountain biker? Or between a Formula 1 driver and a rally driver?

Maybe, in general, you see a lot of similarities. All the athletes in these comparisons should be disciplined, train a lot, eat healthily, be mentally and physically in top shape, have good equipment, and so on. Yet, there is an important difference. The first of each pair focuses on a predictable and known course. The one who performs as efficiently and quickly as possible is the winner. A prior strategy can be formulated. The second, however, has a very different challenge. He has to deal with unexpected events and changing circumstances. This requires anticipation and improvisation. The person who responds the quickest and is the most flexible is the winner.

Also, something else interesting is going on. The first of the two would fail completely if he went onto the course of the second. A rowing scull would sink immediately on a white-water river. A specialist 5,000-meter speed skater couldn't keep up in a hockey game. A road bike is unusable on bumpy mountain trails or loose sand. And Max Verstappen's Formula 1 car would be useless in the Paris-Dakar. Conversely, though, the second athlete is often very capable at the sport of the first, and can deliver acceptable performance. He can adjust; he is more of an all-rounder than the first.

Now, if you take a look at your own organization, can you see it as an elite athlete? And if so, which of the two types of athletes? How well does it adapt to unexpected events and changing circumstances? How fast, flexible, and agile is it? How smart and nimble? How well does the organization anticipate and improvise? Is it a survivor?

These questions concern us, and, therefore, are central to this book. Here is a guide to how the book approaches these issues.

1.2   Accelerate

Changes in market conditions, in the approach of competitors, in the needs of customers, and within your own organization are going ever faster and deeper. And for many organizations, this is an enormous struggle. Most are unable to adapt, fully or quickly enough, to the circumstances. They lack resilience. It is a regular complaint of many executives that their organization simply cannot maintain such a breakneck pace.

They are under a tremendous risk, because it is their actual existence that is endangered. They either adapt or they die. Darwin demonstrated this for flora and fauna, but this does not only apply to organisms, but also to organizations. As you will read later in this book, there are massive dynamics in the creation, growth, shrinking, and disappearing of organizations. There are more and more start-ups, but, as a rule-of-thumb, 90 percent are gone again within five years. The number of bankruptcies and liquidations has been rising for a long time, well before the financial crisis. This doesn't only apply to small businesses, but also global icons like Nokia, Saab, and Kodak. To use a travel metaphor, these organizations were on a train to a fixed destination, when they really needed to be out exploring.

At the same time, there are many examples of companies reinventing themselves, such as Apple, LEGO, and Mini. And examples of companies that emerged from nowhere and through searching found their raison d'être: companies like Amazon, TomTom, and easyJet.

The question is how you can ensure that your organization will be a winner in tomorrow's market. It turns out that agility plays a crucial role. As you'll soon see, agility embraces flexibility and maneuverability. Adaptability is key. Literally translated, agility means the ability to move quickly and easily. Within the context of this book, it encompasses terms like lightness, speed, sharpness, strength, focus, and precision. The aim of agility is adaptivity, the responsive capacity of the organization to adapt flexibly to new requirements. There is an unmistakable *need for speed*. Everything revolves around minimizing time-to-market.

It might help to compare it with driving. Firstly, looking at traffic flows, you can see a big difference in the agility and responsiveness of lorries and buses compared with cars and motorcycles. Secondly, driving a car is a dynamic process; it is impossible to prepare for everything. Also, it makes no sense to learn all the roads and their traffic rules by heart. Because traffic is just like a flock of birds, a complex chaos of interacting road users sometimes do very unexpected things. Moreover, there are road works, countless new roads, and diversions, and so on. So, you get your driving license on the basis of standard, existing criteria. Driving lessons begin with the theory. By studying traffic rules, you get insight into how road users should interact with each other, how you should behave, and how you can recognize certain traffic situations. Then you go on to practice these, until whatever the traffic throws at you, you are able to apply insight and agility, so you can always respond quickly and appropriately. You do this, of course, by continually looking around you, choosing the right direction, monitoring your dashboard, and, where possible, anticipating. And on you go in this continuous process. You accelerate, change gear, brake, use the lights, horn, and turn signals, so you can drive smoothly in any traffic situation. In one word, you are improvising. In the beginning, it is a bit rough (the insurance companies know all about that), but once you've got enough miles under your belt, you get faster and better. Eventually, it becomes second nature; you do it intuitively and, perhaps worryingly, realize that sometimes you've been on "autopilot."

And this is how you want it to be in your organization. This is the essence of agile management.

1.3   Agile Management: In Theory and Practice

Agile management trusts that the process will deliver the desired agility and through this, the necessary adaptability. Increasingly, executives want to make their organizations agile, but do not know how to. Or they have already taken their first steps and are wondering how they can roll out the approach or make it more professional; these are the people for whom this book is especially intended.

It is understandable that for many people, agile carries the connotation of software development, because they know that is the origin of agile-development approaches such as Scrum. For some time now, however, this approach has had a much wider application: in engineering, product development, research, marketing, and project management of all kinds. The approach, in principle with a little customization where appropriate, can be applied in most parts of the organization, and not just in commercial enterprises. It fits well within nearly any kind of organization, including (semi)governmental and nonprofit, internal and external customers, services, products, channels, processes, and so on.

But agility goes further than that: it pertains to factors such as customers, strategy, business models and propositions, leadership, culture, staffing, systems, processes, information, collaboration, experimenting, metrics, and more. And that's what this book is all about. It examines the full breadth of agility and does so from two perspectives. Part one offers theoretical insights to understand the relevance of agility to your organization. It uses real examples to explain why change is happening so frequently and increasingly at fundamental levels. It also tells you how to anticipate change and how agility thinking started. You will see that it is applicable in the majority of situations you might encounter. You will learn why experimentation and failure are important and what are the other principles upon which agile management is based.

Are you more a hands-on person, interested less in theory and more in practice? Then you can go directly to part two, where you'll find how to translate agile principles specifically for use in your daily work or practice. To begin with, you can determine precisely how agile your organization currently is. Then you can read how to structure your organization and processes to maximize agility. What continuously repeating steps constitute these processes? What tools help in completing those steps and in what ways? This approach and the associated tools have been developed by combining experimental practice with existing methods and supplementing it with new solutions.

The individual chapters are explained below; a kind of navigation system when reading this book.

Topics per Chapter

In Chapter 2, you learn about Darwinism. You see that every organization has to adapt to changing circumstances, otherwise it runs the very great risk of becoming extinct. Also, you will see that agile organizations are the most successful in adapting to these changes, and so perform better.

Chapter 3 looks more deeply into changing circumstances, both externally and internally. You see that more is changing, more rapidly and more deeply, and agility is required in order to create and maintain the necessary adaptability. Unfortunately, many organizations come up short due to resistance, lack of internal cooperation, and fear of failure.

The idea that it is vital for agility that trying and failing are allowed and accepted is central to Chapter 4. You learn why it is essential, as early as possible in the process, to try and fail as often as you can. You can find inspiration in wonderful examples of valuable inventions that were discovered accidentally.

In Chapter 5, you will discover that agility also makes the decisive difference in situations where winning is crucial, like warfare and elite sports, and Chapter 6 gives you the opportunity to delve deeper into the history of agile management. You will see that the approach is not a flash in the pan, but more than a hundred years in development. You can also read about the benefits and efficiency of agile management.

Chapter 7 discusses the agile-management approach in detail, examining the eight principles on which the approach is based, such as value creation, alignment, and empowerment. It also describes how agile management can be used for both internal and external customers. The chapter ends by looking at the importance of IT.

The practical part of this book (Part 2) begins at Chapter 8. First of all, you can do a quick self-assessment to determine how agile your own organization really is. Then it discusses where your organization should focus and what this means for leadership. Finally, there is an extensive case study of ING Bank.

The process central to agile management is explained in Chapter 9. There you will see that this includes three continuously repeating steps: *Think–Do–Learn*. These steps are further explored in subsequent chapters.

Chapters 10 and 11 cover the first step: *Think*. They go into how to best monitor changes in circumstances and how to quickly adapt your business model, both internally and externally. You learn how to make your organization more customer-focused. How to become smarter at prioritization and planning your improvements and to make use of hypotheses and metrics.

In Chapter 12, you go on to the next step: *Do*. An answer to the question of how to design and build value propositions and customer experiences in a quick and practical way, in which you learn how a so-called *minimum viable product* works and how you can test this.

The final step, *Learn*, is the subject of Chapter 13. Here you learn how to analyze your efforts and the results they have delivered. You'll become familiar with the different sources of information that you need for your analysis, what I call the *voice of the customer*. You also learn how to evaluate and pivot.

The last part of the book, from Chapter 14 onwards, addresses the question of how you become future-proof. It contains a summary of everything you have learned, how it all fits together, and discusses how to make real the transformation from your current situation to an agile organization. In addition, you will find answers to frequently asked questions arising from real-world practice and references to inspiring resources for supportive background information.

By reading this chapter, you'll have discovered the following:
- *You can look at organizations in different ways. One is to assess the level of agility. Agility is required for adaptivity: the extent to which organizations can adapt to changes in internal or external conditions.*

- *Agile management is an approach that facilitates this for the entire organization. The approach is not just limited to IT, but also includes many more aspects than just product development, for example. Agile management applies to both internal and external customers and is applicable in almost any kind of organization.*
- *The book teaches you two ways to apply agile management within your organization: first, by introducing you to the theoretical background and then letting you discover how you can make it a concrete part of your organization's business practice.*

PART 1

Treasure hunt! Searching for the Essence of Agile Management

On Expedition!

In part 1, you will discover what agile management means. I use many examples from theory and practice to discuss what agile management is and is not. This section provides answers to questions like:

- What is adaptivity and why is it relevant to my organization?
- Why is more and more changing, inside and outside my organization, and how can I better anticipate this?
- Why can't I get my organization to adapt quickly to changing circumstances?
- What is the importance of experimentation and how should I work with failures?
- What are the origins of agile management?
- What are good examples of agile organizations from which I can learn?
- What are the key principles of agile management and how does it actually work?
- Isn't it really only good for software developers?
- How can I use it for my internal and external customers?
- And why are data and information so important to agile management?

CHAPTER 2

Adaptivity—Adapt or Die

Change is the law of life. And those who look only to
the past or present are certain to miss the future.
—John F. Kennedy

Every organization—whether commercial or nonprofit, start-up or well-established—will, sooner or later, have to deal with changes to its internal or external circumstances. In this chapter, we take a trip into nature to understand why it is so important to be able to adapt to change. You can also read about organizations that experienced major changes, with fatal consequences.

2.1 A (R)evolutionary Idea from an Amateur Biologist

A sailing ship drops anchor in the bay of a beautiful island. A moment later, its dinghy is carrying a young man to the shore. After four long and hard years, sharing a small cabin with a captain suffering from melancholy and fits of rage, he is looking forward to the prospect, once more, of heading out alone.

The young man answers to the name Charles Darwin and 26 years earlier was born in Shrewsbury, a quiet village in the West Midlands of England. His mother—who dies when Charles is eightcomes from the rich Wedgwood family, makers of the famous porcelain. His father, a prosperous physician who sees Charles as his successor, is terribly disappointed when, at the age of sixteen, he abruptly stops his medical studies because he cannot stand the sight of blood. After another failure, this time studying law, he finally sees a chance to graduate in theology at Cambridge, with a boring life in a rural parish as his future. But his great passion is biology.

When in the spring of 1831, he gets the offer to sail on the research ship HMS Beagle, he does not have to think for long. The captain, Robert FitzRoy, is looking for a dinner companion because, in his position, he may only invite "gentlemen" and his favorite companion has cancelled at the last minute. FitzRoy, an extremely strange man, chooses Darwin partly because of the shape of his nose, which, to FitzRoy, indicates a strong character. That Darwin was trained as a cleric adds to FitzRoy's conviction. FitzRoy's official mission is, indeed, to map the coastal waters, but his hobby is to look for evidence for the biblical interpretation of creation. On departing from Plymouth, on December 27th, 1831, he could never have suspected that this expedition would result in evidence precisely to the contrary.

It's September 17th, 1835 when Darwin sets foot ashore in Chatham, the easternmost island of the Galapagos archipelago, about 800 kilometers off the coast of Ecuador. During the ensuing five weeks, he collects from the group of islands a huge collection of specimens of the local flora and fauna, including many different types of finches. Darwin was not yet an accomplished naturalist, so a few obvious observations completely elude him at the time. Being inexperienced he also forgets to document from which islands the birds come. It will take another two years, after returning, to sort out this mess completely.

Coping

Darwin's friend John Gould, an ornithologist, notices, in 1837, that in addition to their obvious similarities, the finches also have very different beaks. Together, they then determine thirteen different species, and assume that the beak of each species is adapted to the local food sources of their respective island. Their conclusion is that the birds were not created this way, but they have, in some way, changed themselves. This was probably pretty bad news for the creationist FitzRoy.

Six years after returning, Darwin finally begins to work out his new theory in a manuscript. In 1844, he lays it aside as the book *Vestiges of the Natural History of Creation* appears. It suggests that man might well have evolved from lower primates, without help from the Divine Creator. There is a tremendous uproar and the anonymous author is cursed from the pulpits. (For that reason, the author waited forty years before he dared to let his name be known; it turned out to be Robert Chambers, the largest bible publisher in the world). Darwin decided to devote himself to raising ten children and writing a rather-thick tome about barnacles (which, understandably, he later hated) that kept him busy for eight years. He also became a kind of recluse, barely able to work because he was suffering from the debilitating effects of Chagas disease, which he contracted in South America as a result of an insect bite.

A Controversial Theory

Darwin's manuscript would probably have been lost if he had not received a request, in 1858, from Alfred Russell Wallace to comment on his essay. This essay bore strong similarities to Darwin's manuscript. Darwin then decided that they had to present their theory jointly to the Linnaean Society. Wallace lost interest and, from then on, would refer to this theory as "Darwinism."

Finally, toward the end of 1859, *On the Origin of Species* is published, in which Darwin presents his theory. It is an immediate commercial success, although there is much criticism in the early years about there being only limited evidence. However, in 1865, the Czech monk Gregor Mendel, published evidence of a mechanism that explained how, according to Darwin, all living things are descended from a single common source. Nevertheless, Darwin's theory was not widely accepted until 1930. During his later life, Darwin was frequently honored by the scientific community, but never for his evolutionary theory.[1]

By the way, Darwin never used the phrase *survival of the fittest*; it is taken from the book *Principles of Biology*, written by Herbert Spender in 1864. The term *evolution* was first used by Darwin in 1872, in the sixth edition of his book. But what was in his first edition is the now famous phrase:

It is not the strongest of the species that survives, nor the most intelligent; but the one most adaptable to change.

This phrase summarizes very strongly what Darwin understood. That the animal kingdom is all about one thing: adaptivity. According to him, the ability of species to adapt to (changing) circumstances is the most important condition to survive natural selection.

You will probably wonder what this trip to the wonderful world of flora and fauna has to do with your organization? More than you think. Let's go on an expedition into the world of organizations and find out.

2.2   From Organisms to Organizations: The Extinction of Technology Companies

What is the brand of your current mobile phone? The probability is now very small that it is a Nokia. But have you ever had a Nokia phone in the past? Probably the answer is affirmative. Strange, is it not? You'll soon see what is the logical explanation for this.

Many, including perhaps yourself, seem inclined to think that the biggest companies will always win, meaning that well-known brand names would exist forever. But, if you look at the stock market listings on Wall Street over the past fifty years, you'll make a surprising discovery. What do titans like Kodak, Polaroid, Chrysler, GM, Saab, Rover, Pan Am, RCA, Compaq, Atari, MGM, and Texaco have in common? They needed state aid, or had to be taken over, have been decimated, were consigned to the margins, or have gone bankrupt. Let's look at a few of these examples.

Eastman Kodak

Founded in 1888 by George Eastman, Kodak hits its peak about a century later. The company then had over 145,000 employees worldwide, generating more than $16 billion in annual sales and was valued at approximately $30 billion. It is so ubiquitous that even its slogan is found in most dictionaries: *a Kodak moment*. Neil Armstrong, the first man on the moon, used Kodak film when he made his famous recordings. More than eighty films that have won an Oscar for best film were made with Kodak film. Kodak was a stock market icon on Wall Street, an example of the American Dream. But then two things happened. First, Fuji entered the US market and brought a smart marketing approach that rapidly grew their market share to 17 percent. Second, Kodak decided to hold fire on digital photography (Kodak had already invented the first digital camera in 1975 and registered 1,100 patents, but chose not to put the camera into production because it would harm its film business). Only at the beginning of the new millennium, as film revenues collapsed, was it given any priority. For several years, Kodak then benefitted, thanks to aggressive marketing, from the rapid and profitable growth in sales of digital cameras.

But, the company does not anticipate that these cameras will quickly become commodities, or that this, together with the arrival of newcomers from Asia, will force prices down, creating negative margins for Kodak. Market share falls from 27 percent to 7 percent and the losses build up fast. In 2012, the company files for bankruptcy, making a $1.3 billion dollar loss on annual revenues of $4.1 billion. After selling almost all its patents, Kodak is now trying to survive as a supplier of printing products in the enterprise market. As Steve Ballamy put it in 2015: "We were a bankrupt company three years ago, and now we're kind of a start-up. But we're like the most mature start-up in the history of business." Current market capitalization hovers around $660 million, around 2 percent of its peak value. Let's just hope that your pension fund has not invested in Kodak.

Nokia and Others

Or take another giant, Nokia. It was founded in 1865 to make rubber overshoes. Around 1980, they decided to deploy a bold diversification strategy by focusing on a new product in the emerging market of mobile phones. This makes the company extremely successful. Between 1998 and 2012, Nokia is the world leader in this market, selling, in 2005, its billionth phone. At its height, Nokia has sales of $37 billion, employs 132,000 workers and has a market capitalization of $251 billion.

Although rumors are rife in 2002, it's not until January 2007 that Nokia has its *deus ex machina* moment: the totally unexpected

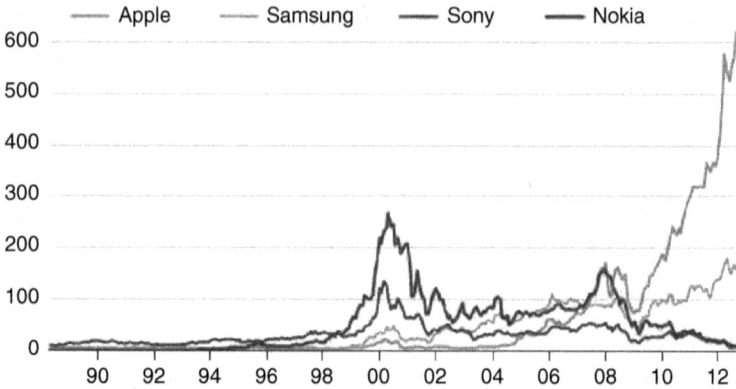

Figure 2.1 The market capitalization of Nokia and its direct competitors: after the collapse of the "Internet bubble" in 2000, the demise of Nokia becomes final in 2007; Sony is also struggling despite the success of its PlayStation (Source: Thomson Reuters Datastream)

introduction by Apple of the iPhone (see Figure 2.1). Samsung responds almost immediately with its F700. Nokia's leadership sees this as a disruptive innovation because they think they are way ahead in the field of hardware and software (Nokia even already have a successful smartphone, the Communicator, but not one with a touchscreen and apps). Grown lethargic and cumbersome via many years of success, Nokia's time-to-market for innovations from the R&D labs is much too long. Due to conservative internal forces, the company is not sufficiently open to change. When a member of the Board of Directors takes the new iPhone home one evening, his four-year daughter begins immediately to play with it. When, after a while, she asks him if she can put the "magic" phone under her pillow, he realizes that his company has a huge problem.[2]

Toward the end of 2008, Nokia finally introduces its first touchscreen phone, the 5800 XpressMusic. However, this just does not function well. Moreover, Apple and Google have been a lot smarter than Nokia, working with app developers. Mobile-app programming is easier, apps offer increased revenues, and both offer a central download store (App Store and Android Market). Until 2010, Nokia's smartphone sales continue to grow, but the overall market is growing many times faster. Despite hefty price cuts, sales collapse. Although the company still sells a lot of classical phones, intense competition and the associated price erosion of 60 percent eat too much of its margin. In 2013, Nokia is technically bankrupt and is forced to sell its Mobile Division and related patents to Microsoft for only $7.4 billion (who then decided to totally discontinue the Nokia brand in November 2016). The crown jewels for a pittance, because Nokia simply did not have the necessary resilience. And probably no one at Nokia was rejoicing at the prospect of making rubber wellys again.

Research In Motion, the manufacturer of BlackBerry, had a similar experience. This company trusted blindly that its large installed base, its own network, and its superior security capabilities would allow it to continue to dominate the market. As a result, Research In Motion was too slow in adapting to changes in the market and its market share fell, between 2010 and 2016, from 41 percent to 1 percent. Its market capitalization is now about one-twentieth of at its peak.

Even successful dotcom pioneer Yahoo! proved vulnerable. It was founded in 1994 and became an immensely popular web portal, with a market cap of about 110 billion dollars in 1999. But when the Internet grew, a search engine became a necessary tool for Internet users. Yahoo! decided not to build its own, but to use the search engine of start-up Google, thus helping its own rival become a dominant player. In later years, the company experienced trouble in finding the right strategic focus, resulting in 24 different mission statements during its lifetime. This also inhibited a successful acquisition policy. In 2002 Yahoo! was offered the opportunity to buy Google for 1 billion dollars and in 2006 to buy Facebook for 1.1 billion dollars, but declined in both cases. It did buy companies like Flickr, GeoCities, Delicious, and Tumblr, but these all quietly faded away. In 2008, it received a take-over bid of 44.6 billion dollars from Microsoft, but did not accept it. In recent years, Yahoo has tried to position itself as a broad media company, but it really missed out on the growth of mobile Internet, partly by refusing to build its own browser or operating system. In July 2016, Yahoo! was forced to sell all of its Internet activities to Verizon Communications. As they will rebrand these activities as Altaba, this means the end of an illustrious company.[3]

When Kodak and Nokia were at their heights, who would have dared predict the total collapse of the absolute market leaders? Pretty much anyone who did would have been declared insane. But both could not adapt enough or quickly, could not cope with changing circumstances. But this happens not only to large, established companies. As you'll see below, it also applies to start-ups.

Iridium

In 1991, Motorola and a global partnership of eighteen companies decided to build a mobile phone system that could be used anywhere in the world. Literally anywhere. From the glaciers of Antarctica to a ship in the middle of the ocean; the peaks of the Himalayas to the heart of the African jungle. They dared to think big. No less than $5.2 billion was invested in an arsenal of fifteen rockets from the United States, China, and Russia. These were needed to put a fleet of 72 satellites into orbit, 781 kilometers above the earth's surface. Seven years after the company was founded, all the satellites were, at last, in orbit and the first call was made. And not quite nine months later, the company went into receivership.

What went wrong exactly? In 1991, there was no complete global coverage for mobile phones and the available coverage was also expensive and unreliable. On this basis, Iridium made several assumptions about the needs of potential customers, what would be appropriate products and services, and of course potential earnings. But in the seven years it took to bring their product to market, innovation in mobile phones and mobile networks developed incredibly fast. Coverage had become much better, call rates had reduced significantly, and the first data applications were already available. In addition, the phones themselves had become much smaller, while those of Iridium were about the size and weight of a brick (an old military field telephone had nothing on these). Even worse, the Iridium telephone could not be used in a building or car, because it needed a *line-of-sight* connection to a satellite—not exactly practical. A conversation with a regular cell phone cost (in 1998) about 50 cents per minute and with an Iridium phone 7 dollars. The purchase price of the device itself was over $3,000. So, day-by-day, Iridium's target customer segment shrank, until there remained just one, very small, niche market. Looking on the bright side, however, at least Iridium didn't have to invest in an expensive CRM system.

Incidentally, Iridium is once more alive and kicking. In 2000, an investment group bought the total Iridium Estate for $25 million; its "real" value was around $6 billion. In 2011, with an adapted business model, the new company welcomed its 500,000th customer.[4]

How It Can Also Be

Happily, despite the dramatic example of Iridium, new businesses are continuously being created, and becoming successful. Think of online start-ups: names like Alibaba, Amazon, Facebook, Google, WhatsApp, Instagram, Snapchat, Spotify, Zappos, Uber, and Zalando. And other companies such as Tesla, Dyson, GoPro, Intel, ASML, Dell, TomTom, Ikea, Swatch, easyJet, Smart, Cirque du Soleil, and Oculus Rift. And there are large established companies that have been forced to reinvent themselves and have done so quite successfully. LEGO, Marks & Spencer, Burberry, Mini, Apple, and Club Med all did so. Of all these companies, you could say that they are sufficiently adaptive, because they saw changes and then took action.

But would you dare to bet your savings against them still existing in 25 years? And what might the future look like for nonprofit organizations such as hospitals, Chambers of Commerce, museums, charities, water boards, pension funds, unions, and municipalities? Interesting food for thought perhaps?

2.3   Future-Proofing: Agility Required

The parallel between organisms and organizations is evident. In Darwin's terms, organizations such as Kodak, Nokia, and Iridium have not survived *natural selection*. They are extinct, just like the mammoth, the cave bear, or saber-toothed tiger. Various case studies indicate that this mainly has to do with a lack of adaptivity. Not surprising when you consider the increasing speed in which their environments developed. We also see, for example, that the number of patent applications, the annual number of shares traded, and the volumes of data used by companies also show exponential growth curves since circa 1980.[5] Can we recognize these patterns in other organizations? That's what we are going to look at now.

Birth and Death

There are many well-known examples of companies that have existed for more than a century: Ford, Harley-Davidson, DuPont, 3M, Siemens, General Electric, Heineken, and Philips (in 2006, after almost 1,400 years in business, the oldest company in the world closed down: the Japanese temple-builder Kongo Kumi). However, these companies are the exception, not the rule. There is tremendous dynamism in the creation, growth, shrinking, and disappearing of companies.

Let's first look at emergence and disappearance, the coming and going of businesses. According to The Organisation for Economic Co-operation and Development (OECD) statistics on their 28 member countries, the period from 1998 to 2015 was somewhat cyclical, seeing the economy both grow and contract. In this period, an increasing number of businesses were established annually (including 26 percent being subsidiaries of existing companies), with an average yearly growth of nearly 6 percent. However, the number of businesses that closed (including 9 percent bankruptcies) also increased, with an average yearly growth of over 5 percent. Ultimately, the numbers show that, overall, there is growth, but when we look at company size, the picture is far more nuanced. The number of businesses with 50 or more employees has decreased by over 5 percent, and those with 2 to 49 employees have remained relatively constant; the number with just one employee (the self-employed) grew by 29 percent. The average life expectancy of a new business, at present, has risen to about six years, with 66 percent closing down within their first six years of existence.[6]

Just look for a moment at the battlefield of retail where, in recent years, the traditional players had no response to the rapid rise of e-commerce and other changes. For example, Blockbuster, Circuit City, RadioShack, Dixons, Woolworths, Ritz, Tower Records, Comet, Borders, Athena, Tie Rack, Zavvi, Austin Reed, BHS, Thirst Quench, Dewhurst, and American Apparel all went bankrupt. (And for how long will a store like Barnes & Noble still exist, not to mention small players like independent local stores).

Growth and Shrinkage

Now, let's look at the growth and shrinkage of the financial turnover of companies. Since 1955, *Fortune* magazine has been publishing its ranking of the largest US companies, based on revenue, the *Fortune 500*. Studying the rankings over longer periods provides some interesting insights. For example, in these sixty years, only four companies have been top more than once: General Motors (37 times), ExxonMobil (ten times), Wal-Mart (four times), and Shell Oil (the American branch of Shell) twice. But what about the durability of the other companies on the list?

Here, too, it is very dynamic. As Figure 2.2 shows, every ten years, on average, about half of the companies fall out of the list. This is due to shrinkage in the turnover of these companies, and increased turnover of companies, which were previously outside the *Fortune* 500.[7] Other research confirms this: of the companies in the Fortune 500 list of 1955, only 12.2 percent were still in the list in 2014.[8] Babson Olin even expects that, in the next decade, 40 percent of existing Fortune 500 companies will not survive, while Yale estimates that the average lifespan of S&P 500 companies has decreased to fifteen years, from sixty to -seven years in the 1920s.[9]

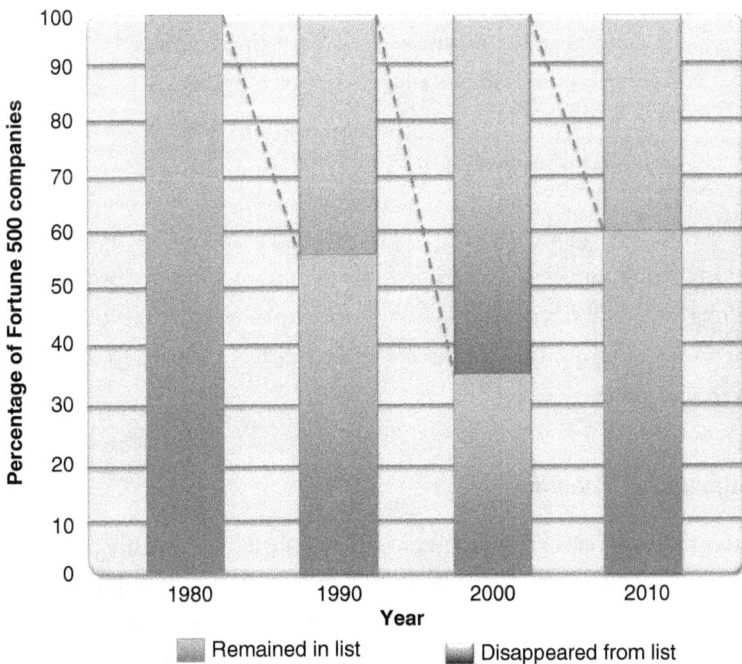

Figure 2.2 On average, around half of the companies fall out of the Fortune 500 within ten years

That the turnover of large companies rises and falls is clear. But what about smaller companies? Dartmouth researched all 29,688 companies listed on US stock markets from 1960 to 2009 in 10-year cohorts and concluded that longevity is decreasing. Companies that listed before 1970 had a 92 percent chance of surviving the next five years, whereas companies that listed from 2000 to 2009 had only a 63 percent chance, even when controlled for the dotcom bust and multiple periods of recession.[10] The World Bank noted that in the period 2006 to 2014, more companies suffered a decline in sales and the number of fast-growing companies fell. That seems logical, given the prolonged economic crisis. But how does the picture look over a longer period? To determine this, US scientists used the renowned Compustat database and looked at turnover and profitability in the period 1980 to 2012, a period in which there were frequent, and strong changes in market conditions.

They discovered a very clear, established pattern of performance:

- 18 percent of companies outperformed their industry average 80 percent or more of the time;
- 13 percent of companies underperformed compared to their industry average 80 percent or more of the time;
- 69 percent of companies exhibited erratic periods of over- and underperformance within their industry.

Most companies, therefore, perform very erratically or relatively poorly. The number of companies able to sustain good performance for a long time is limited. And only a few companies managed to improve themselves, during the measurement period, from erratic to long-term overperformer*s.*

Adjustment Potential

Does this dynamic of development, growing, shrinking, and disappearance of firms tell us something about the extent to which companies are able to adapt to their circumstances? According to the researchers, that is indeed the case. They found overperformers possess the skills to adapt quickly to their environment, to see and react earlier than their competitors, exploiting opportunities and responding quickly to threats. Other research also shows that 61 percent of the fast-growing companies, at least once, radically changed course. For example, by jumping into an emerging market or creating a new business model. In short, it is all about *agility*.

By now, you'll have the suspicion that the success of your organization might well depend on the manner in which your organization works with future changes in its circumstances. Therefore, in the following section you can find out more about the causes and impact of these changes.

By reading this chapter, you'll have discovered the following:
- *Scientific research has shown that only those animals and plants that can adapt to changing circumstances survive.*
- *This adaptivity is required in order to avoid extinction, and applies not only to organisms, but also to organizations. Kodak, Nokia, and Iridium are negative examples of this concept.*
- *There is a lot of momentum in the creation, growth, shrinking, and disappearance of companies. Scientific research shows that the best-performing organizations are agile, allowing them to adapt quickly to change.*

References

1. Bryson, B. (2003). *A Short History of Nearly Everything*. New York: Random House.
2. Wokke, A. (2014). *A Goodbye to Nokia; Goodbye to a Former Leader*. Tweakers.
3. Cohen, R. (2017). *Yahoo Article*. FD.
4. Blank, S., and B. Dorf. (2012). *The Startup Owner Manual*. K & S Ranch Press.
5. Kotter, J. (2014). *Accelerate*. Brighton: Harvard Business Review Press.
6. Stat Line–CBS.
7. Worley, C. G., T. Williams, and E. D. Lawler. (2014). *The Agility Factor*. San Francisco: Jossey-Bass.

8. Perry, M. J. (2014). *Fortune 500 Firms in 1955 vs. 2014; 88% are Gone, and We're All Better off Because of that Dynamic "Creative Destruction."* AEI blog.

9. Ismail, S., S. M. Malone, and Y. van Geest. (2014). *Exponential Organizations*. New York: Diversion Publishing.

10. Govindarajan, V., and A. Srivastava. (2016). "The Scary Truth about Corporate Survival." *Harvard Business Review*, December issue, pp. 24–25.

CHAPTER 3

Nothing is Permanent Except Change

Have no fear of perfection; you'll never reach it.
—Salvador Dali

As you saw in Chapter 2, many organizations are not agile enough. They are struggling to adapt to changing circumstances, which often threaten their existence. In Chapter 3, you will discover the causes of these changing conditions and why it is often difficult to deal with them.

3.1 Change is a Constant

"Nothing is permanent except change." These wise words were expressed by the Greek philosopher Heraclitus around 500 BC. Now, 2,500 years later, it appears that change is indeed still something we have to deal with constantly, and within organizations. That is confirmed by various, annual, large-scale studies conducted among CEOs worldwide. They are asked to identify the most important issues on their agendas for the foreseeable future.[1] Although there are obvious differences in study approaches, there remains, in recent years, a clear common thread running through the responses.

CEOs see that

- market conditions are increasingly changing;
- developments in information technology are making the playing field faster and more complex;
- speed of change in digital environments is much higher than in traditional offline environments;
- there is always more competition;

- it is becoming increasingly difficult to keep a sustainable competitive advantage over the longer term;
- unexpected new entrants, with disruptive business models, change the market fundamentally and permanently;
- continuous innovation is needed to remain customer-relevant in the future; and
- data are a strategic weapon in the competitive struggle.

In short, plenty of challenges. The CEOs are—rightly—concerned about how their organization can survive in the future. In addition, they also indicate that the time horizon of their strategy planning gets ever closer, because changes are occurring ever more rapidly. They are very ambivalent about these changes, because the momentum of change is growing and many of the issues are interrelated. This makes predicting future scenarios increasingly difficult. It's not for nothing that Mark Twain once said: "It is difficult to make predictions, especially about the future."

VUCA

This problem is also referred to by the term VUCA, an acronym derived from the US Army and used to assess combat situations in terms of their *volatility, uncertainty, complexity,* and *ambiguity.*[2] This concept has been adopted within public and private organizations to assess developments in their current and future contexts. But how do you know if you're dealing with a high(er) degree of VUCA? The four factors can be described as follows (see also Figure 3.1):

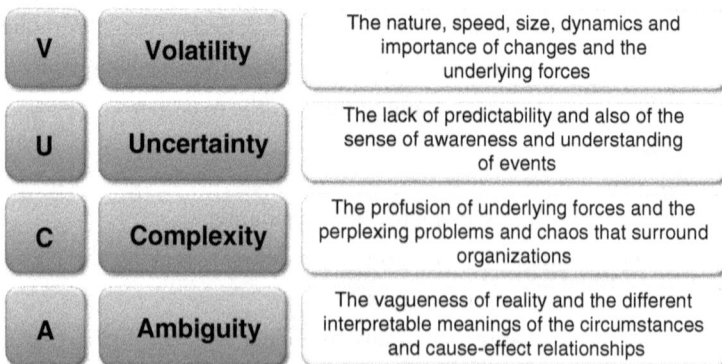

V	Volatility	The nature, speed, size, dynamics and importance of changes and the underlying forces
U	Uncertainty	The lack of predictability and also of the sense of awareness and understanding of events
C	Complexity	The profusion of underlying forces and the perplexing problems and chaos that surround organizations
A	Ambiguity	The vagueness of reality and the different interpretable meanings of the circumstances and cause-effect relationships

Figure 3.1 The VUCA factors limit the possibilities of strategy planning

- *Volatility*—The established order is changed or is in a mess. The unexpected happens, and the opposite happens to that which you would have expected. New concepts appear and you are unsure if they are correct and relevant, and you're wondering if and how to apply them. Old ideas seem not to work anymore.
- *Uncertainty*—You're not sure what is happening or will happen and it affects your self-confidence. You find it increasingly difficult to predict, forecast, and anticipate well. The result is that it becomes very difficult to prepare adequately and appropriately and keep things under control.
- *Complexity*—Events appear to have many possible causes. Cause–effect relationships are unclear because the changes seem too complicated to discern, let alone define. This disorder is complicated by the growing number of interdependent factors that are the causative agents.
- *Ambiguity*—For a given situation or change, there are several possibilities of meaning. You're torn between all the alternative interpretations of a situation. It is no longer easy to say if something is good or bad, right or wrong.[3]

The extent to which VUCA factors apply determines the limits and the scope of strategy planning. And these limits appear nowadays to be even more restrictive. The Telegraph Media Group (TMG), for example, experienced this after taking over Hyves at the end of 2010. At the time of the takeover, Hyves was at its peak, with 10 million members, but many had already noticed that the social networking site was losing member activity to the new kid on the block, Facebook. Within months, a quarter of Hyves' users closed their accounts. Soon this change achieved critical mass and, at the end of 2012, Hyves was literally decimated: only 10 percent of the original members were still active. TMG decided to turn Hyves into a gaming site for kids. This has not been a success and, recently, TMG wrote off €43 million.

Change is happening so fast that one might speak not of an era of change, but a change of era. To illustrate this, Figure 3.2 shows how in recent years it took start-ups ever less time to reach the "unicorn" status, a market capitalization of one billion dollars. The exponential decline shows

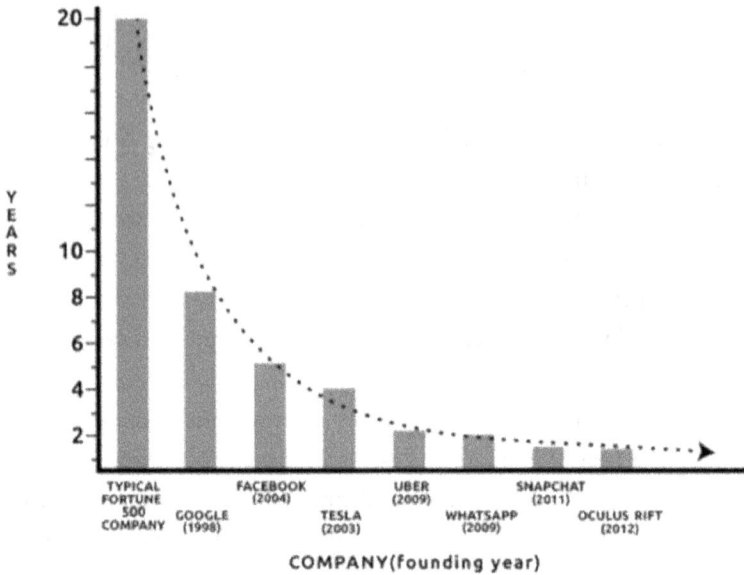

Figure 3.2 The time needed by start-ups to reach the "unicorn" status in recent years

a "double down" speed comparable with that in Moore's Law, which, based on his thirty years of research, Kurzweil adapted into the Law of Accelerating Returns.[4] A comparable effect can be seen in Figure 3.3, which shows how innovations need ever less time to reach 50 million users.[5] So, welcome to the agile age!

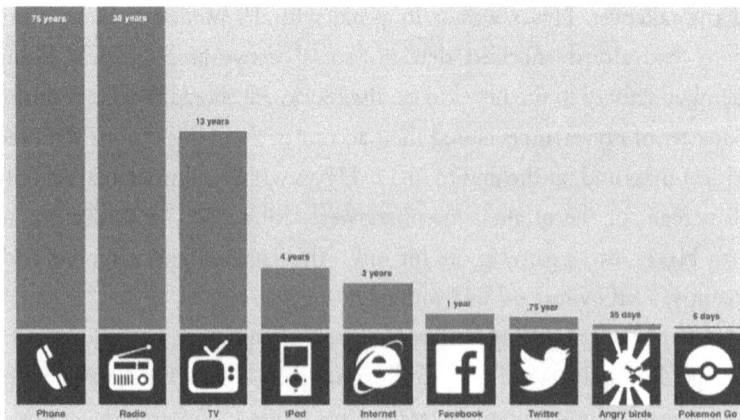

Figure 3.3 The time needed by innovations to reach 50 million users

And, if predicting changing conditions is apparently so difficult, logic implies that organizations must then be very good at "seeing things early" and adapting to changing circumstances as soon as they perceive them. Therefore, it is useful to understand the genesis of change, so you can instantly develop effective solutions. This starts with understanding the factors that are the driving force behind the changes. Consequently, in the next section, we discuss the causes of change.

3.2   The Origins of Change

Changes can be either internal or external. This usually means that internal changes are due to, or in anticipation of, external changes. Therefore, we will look at them separately.

External Changes

Do you still have a video store near where you live? Or a music store around the corner? A printing shop, perhaps? A baker, greengrocer, butcher? Probably not. And when did you last see a bookstore outside of a city center? The disappearance of these retailers has everything to do with what these traders experienced as external changes.

External changes are caused by underlying factors known as "drivers." Within these drivers, we can distinguish eight different categories, set out in the STEEPLED analysis model in Figure 3.4:

1. *Sociocultural*: Social developments, for example manners, public opinion, lifestyle, culture, art, and religion.
2. *Technology*: Innovations in products, processes, and systems and their adoption, including, for example, infrastructure and communications.
3. *Economy*: Changes in the economy and purchasing power through factors such as imports and exports, inflation and price levels, disposable income, income, and consumer confidence.
4. *Environment*: Changes in factors like availability of natural resources, energy, health, environment, nature conservation, and ecology.
5. *Politics*: Policy and influence of both the government and politics on society, such as public order, business environment, and through interventions in the economy.

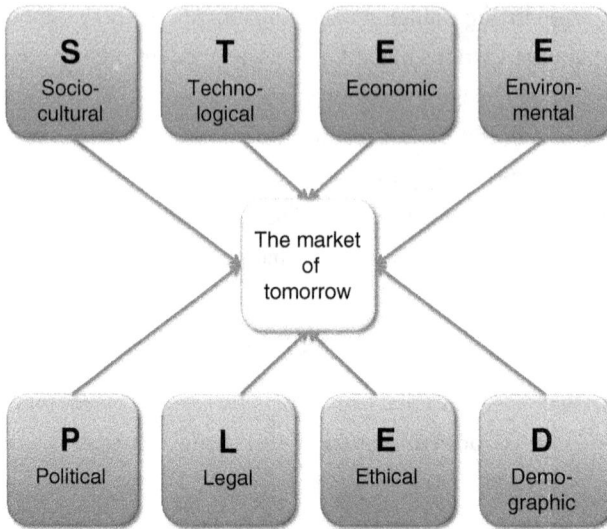

Figure 3.4 Drivers of change in the market

6. *Legislation*: Legal factors such as laws and regulations, as well as the affairs of law enforcement through prosecution, the judiciary, and other qualified authorities.
7. *Ethical*: Ethical and social values of the population (this category is closely linked to category 1, the sociocultural).
8. *Demographic*: Composition and situation of the population; aspects such as size, location, age distribution, sex, race, education level, occupation, and family composition.

When you look through the lens of the STEEPLED model at the examples of Kodak, Nokia, and Iridium (from section 2.2), you immediately see the changes that so challenged these companies were caused by developments in the second driver, *Technology*. This is probably also one of the main drivers of the past 25 years—alongside of course the driver *Economy*, responsible for the enormous impact many markets experienced during the financial crisis of 2008. The driver *Environment* led to changes in the demands of customers and governments in the area of sustainability; much change has been driven by *Legislation* in, for example, the operating practices of banks and insurance companies, and many car manufacturers profited from tax incentives on electric vehicles.

The music industry, too, has endured unprecedented change. The digital revolution was accompanied by a massive reduction in turnover, from $38 billion in 1999 to $16.5 billion in 2012, a staggering 50 percent drop. Not only did turnover reduce, it also started to come from completely different sources. Previously, artists produced a new album and went on tour to promote it. Nowadays, concerts account for more than half of the turnover and albums are released primarily as a marketing tool to sell tickets for concerts. In addition, artists generate income from merchandising, YouTube ads, licenses for television and film productions, iTunes downloads, and royalties for streaming through sites such as Spotify and Internet radio stations.[6]

Something similar happened to the newspaper industry, where revenues declined over the last decade from $44.9 billion to $18.9 billion, due to declining advertising revenues and subscriptions.[7] Publishers are still searching for new online business models, because the print business is no longer tenable. Often, these initiatives have come from outside their industry, such as in the case of Zite, Flipboard, and Feedly.

In general. you can say that the increased importance of agility is, in particular, due to[8]

- technological developments and digitalization making product life-cycles shorter, intellectual property becoming increasingly difficult to defend, and the commoditizing of increasing numbers of products and services;
- global markets shifting more and more economic power to countries like China, India, and other emerging economies;
- hugely increased market transparency due to the explosion of online channels with a consequent increase in the power of the customer; and
- online channels making possible direct interaction and collaboration with customers, suppliers, partners, and colleagues from other departments, accelerating innovation.

Internal Changes

Internal changes are rarely autonomous. Generally, they are a direct or indirect result of external changes that are visible in the market. Internal changes can occur in areas such as structure, processes, systems, staffing,

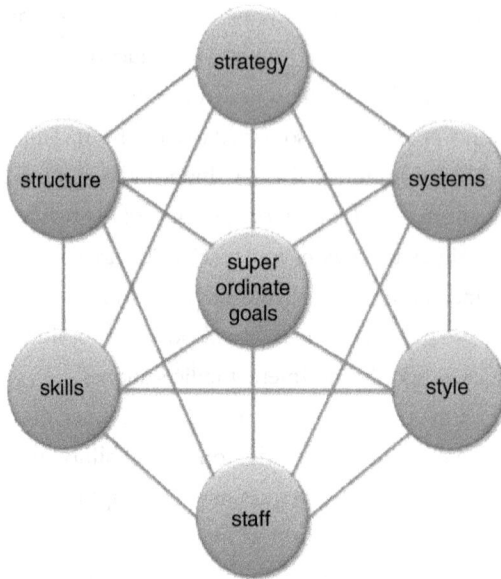

Figure 3.5 The 7S model shows those internal factors that can change[9]

skills, leadership, and culture (see Figure 3.5). These changes are the tangible results of implementing organizational policies. The concrete manifestations of internal changes appear as restructuring, cuts, new IT systems, training, and cultural programs.

The "strategy" factor plays a special role within internal changes: in strategy, the organization determines what it wants to mean in its market and to whom, and how it goes about doing so. The most tangible internal changes become visible if the organization decides to start some of the initiatives found in the famous Ansoff Matrix. This concerns, in particular, the adaptation of existing products or services, offering existing products or services in a new market, or offering new products or services in existing or new markets for the company. These policy decisions are a response to external changes, but can also occur entirely independently.

This approach is not limited explicitly to external customers. Also, departments that service *internal* clients might decide to modify their existing products or services or to offer new products and services. This is because an internal customer will make different demands, on the basis of changes in the 7S model. Or because the changing requirements of external clients filter through to internal departments. This happens when customer-facing departments (such as marketing, sales, and service) translate changing customer needs into their own requirements, which they communicate back along the line to the originating department. For this purpose, we define the internal customer as either "the next process" in the value chain or the specific department receiving the goods or services from the originating department.

Consequences of Changes

The effect of both internal and external changes is that the organization has to adapt to new requirements, which affect both the internal and external activities of the organization, if they are not doing so already. To deal with this, the organization must be adaptive, as can be seen in the lower part of Figure 3.6. In the upper part, we see that the underlying causes of new requirements can be divided into five categories, as discussed above. Within the first two categories, the driver is changes in the business environment:

- changing external conditions, as discussed above with reference to the STEEPLED analysis model;
- changing internal conditions, as discussed via the 7S analysis model.

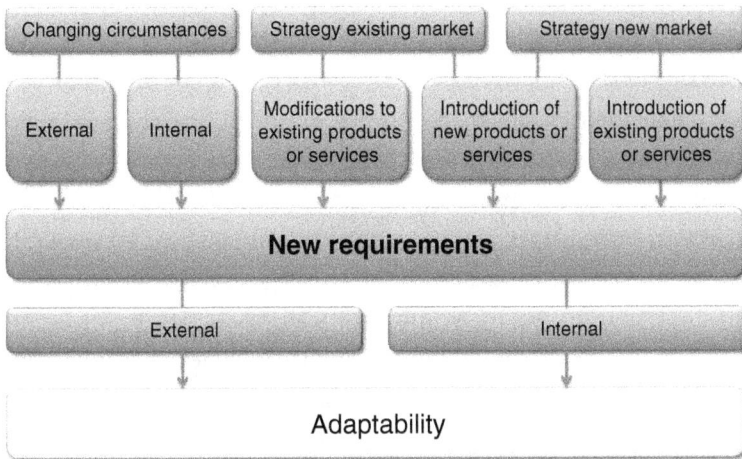

Figure 3.6 Five types of change that ensure the organization must adapt to new internal and/or external requirements

The remaining three categories are of a different sort, namely those triggered by the existing strategic policy. Here, it's about improvement and innovation, whereby it also must be learned how the market will react to a modified or new proposition:

- adapting existing products or services in an existing market;
- introducing new products or services in the current or a new market (as mentioned in the Ansoff Matrix segments *Product Development* and *Diversification*);
- introducing existing products or services into a new market (as mentioned in the Ansoff Matrix segment *Market Development*).

The better you periodically monitor the root causes relevant to change, the faster and more effectively you can anticipate those changes. That plays an important role in agility. But, you will now see why this is so difficult for many organizations.

3.3   Barriers to Adaptivity

Which do you prefer: a long or a short queue? Most likely short. But do you always have the feeling that, somehow, you inevitably choose the wrong line at the supermarket? Or at the toll booths on a highway? In McDonald's or Ikea? Imagine you're in a traffic jam on a road with multiple lanes. What do *you* do? Adjust to the situation by switching from lane to lane, or just sit there? Whatever you choose, the chances are that unintentionally you are confirming Murphy's Law: the person who was next to or behind you is already through. When you're in a queue or traffic jam, this can be painfully obvious.

But if, for example, you want to avoid a traffic jam, by taking the alternative route recommended by your navigation system, then this is not so obvious. Often, when you have made a decision for one route, you have to deal with the nagging feeling that the other route would have been better. You'll never really know. In short, you want your performance (the time you're waiting in line or in traffic) to improve by changing your behavior, but don't really know how to change. That is the way it also works in organizations.

The behavior of organizations such as Kodak, Nokia, and Iridium is, of course, not unique. Most organizations have some degree of difficulty in adapting to changing circumstances. The entrepreneurial network, which made them successful in their initial stages, has transformed into a hierarchical organizational structure that creaks and cracks when faced with the need for rapid change. There are various reasons for this and we'll take a short look at the three most important.

Resistance

Children around seven years old can watch the same movie endlessly (some parents probably know the script of *Frozen* by heart, involuntarily). Psychological research shows that this is because they like predictability and a feeling of being in control. Their mental faculties are usually limited, as is their worldview. Watching or listening, again and again, to something they already know, gives them confirmation of what they already know and a pleasant sense of familiarity. Something similar happens at the table. Most children like to eat and drink what they already know, and don't like tasting new foods or trying new flavors, because they assume that they will not like them.

Sometimes, organizations seem to behave just like young children. They develop repetitive patterns that are hard to break. Changes constitute a potential threat to these routines and are, therefore, often seen in a negative light. This can mean that employees choose, consciously or unconsciously, to ignore changes, or even actively oppose them—you can see it as a particular manifestation of the *fight-or-flight response*.[10] Research also shows that this resistance is often tremendously energy-consuming, which, at best, simply slows down the process and delays the consequences. It is wiser to use the tactics of judo, staying perfectly balanced, waiting to use the energy of the "opponent". As you will see, in Section 7.4, culture and leadership play an important role in this.

Cooperation

Besides this psychological aspect, there is also a "harder" factor at play and it is an important one. Many companies are organized classically, along the lines of structures, systems, and processes. The traditional silo architecture of *line organizations*, based on products, services, or channels, creates obstacles to internal cooperation. But internal cooperation is crucial for the organization to monitor and identify changes holistically, and, on this basis, to initiate the rapid and integrated activities needed to adapt.[11] Lack of internal cooperation leads to a rigid way of working and insufficient resilience to respond quickly and effectively to changes—let alone anticipate them.

Fear of Failure

But yet something else is working here. More and more companies have external shareholders or investors. Especially in the case of a publicly traded company, where the shareholders demand the maximum predictability of results. This forces the leadership to focus increasingly on the short-term, with the consequence that they fail to monitor longer term change. Also, managers and employees often feel that they dare not make mistakes, because they will be punished. Experimentation is thereby seen as too risky, which leads to a culture of choosing the safe course of action, of "looking after the shop." Failure is not an option; people have a compulsion to choose what they know over what they do not: an "idée fixe." This creates a kind of false security. And this isn't just relevant for listed companies, but applies just as well to start-ups, family businesses, and nonprofit organizations.

Recognizable? Fear of failure (Atychiphobia) is so important that we are going to expand on this phenomenon, with the aim of inspiring you.

By reading this chapter, you'll have discovered the following:
- *Levels of volatility, uncertainty, complexity, and ambiguity in the market are getting higher. Competitor and customer behaviors are changing faster and deeper. This shortens the time-period that plans can cover.*
- *Changes take place both internally and externally. This can be monitored with the aid of the STEEPLED and 7S models.*
- *Although many organizations experience changes in their circumstances, they fail to fully adapt because they are not adaptable enough. The main reasons are resistance to change, lack of internal collaboration, and fear of failure.*

References

1. See mckinsey.com, bcg.com, kpmg.com, pwc.com, ibm.com and accenture.com for the various CEO studies.
2. Stiehm, J. H., and N. W. Townsend. (2002). *The J.E.S. Army War College*. Philadelphia: Temple University Press.
3. Horney, N., and T. O'Shea. (2015). *Focused, Fast and Flexible*. Oceanside: Indie Books International.
4. Ismail, S., S. M. Malone, and Y. van Geest. (2014). *Exponential Organizations*. New York: Diversion Publishing.
5. Citi GPS, Technology at Work. (2015); Dobs, No Ordinary Disruption: The Four Global Forces Breaking All the Trends (2016)
6. Pfanner, E. (2013). Music Industry Sales Rise, and Digital Revenue Gets the Credit. *New York Times,* November 22, 2013.
7. Pew Research Center. (2013). *Newspapers: Stabilizing, but Still Threatened—The State of the News Media*. Washington, D.C: Pew Research Center.
8. Setili, A. (2014). *The Agility Advantage*. John Wiley and Sons.
9. Peters, T., and R. H. Waterman. (2005). *In Search of Excellence*. London: Profile Books Ltd.
10. Cannon, W. B. (1932). *Wisdom of the Body*. New York: WW Norton and Company.
11. Hoogveld, M. (2013). *The Excellent Customer Journey Experience*. Amsterdam: Adfogroep.

CHAPTER 4

The Value of Experimenting and Failing

To learn to succeed you must first learn to fail.
—Michael Jordan

In Chapter 3, you already saw that fear of failure inhibits agility. In Chapter 4, we elaborate on this. You will see that experimenting is closely linked to agility. Out of fear of failure, many organizations and their employees experiment infrequently and incompletely, whereas enormously valuable ideas are often the by-products of failure. If you need convincing, a large part of the chapter looks at inspiring examples of "successful" failures.

4.1 Experimentation Is a Powerful Tool

Many clothing manufacturers still produce a new collection at a fixed rate twice a year, for summer and winter. And many clothing stores follow that rhythm. Therefore, there are still cut-price sales, mostly around July and January. Apparel manufacturers cannot do it differently because design, manufacture, and distribution have a very long lead time. Right? Not according to Zara. This clothing chain launches a new collection ten times a year, and also in a unique way. Zara has arranged its production in such a way that it can operate very quickly. This allows the company to produce new garments in small quantities and test them in representative stores. If these garments are sold quickly, Zara can immediately increase manufacturing volumes, and they soon appear in all their stores. The result is that Zara has far less slow-moving stock and has less need of cut-price sales. This increases the profit margins tremendously, so the chain enjoys a very strong competitive position: distinguished design and high quality at a low price. This concept has made founder Amancio Ortega the third-richest man in the world.

The idea of testing is, of course, not new. It has been used for many years by media companies. Take, for example, *Men's Health* magazine. From reader reactions, the editors could see that articles focusing on health topics for their readers' female partners were very popular. On this basis, the publisher (Rodale Press) created a one-off publication to see if there was enough interest to merit a magazine devoted to this genre: *Women's Health*. It sold out immediately and, within a year, circulation was 750,000. Now, besides several other spin-off magazines such as Men's Health Living, Rodale Press also publishes a book series and apps, and through *line and brand extensions,* it keeps testing ways to further capitalize on the brands value. For example with their *Men's Health Box*, containing fitness, nutrition, style, grooming, and tech products.

The same can be seen in television series and talk shows. For instance, The Oprah Winfrey Show was continuously testing whether subjects resonate with the viewer. This could be deduced from the comments on social media and the ratings. On this basis, the producers experimented with spin-offs via pilots, which would be promoted during the show itself. Among others, this resulted in the Dr Phil show, which itself spun-off The Doctors. Some other examples: The Simpsons series are a spin-off from The Tracey Ullman Show; Frasier originated from Cheers; Better Call Saul is derived from Breaking Bad; NCIS from JAG; and Private Practice from Greys Anatomy.

Major film studios tackle this very professionally. Because how do you avoid ending up bankrupt when the film, in which you have invested hundreds of millions of dollars, is a total flop? It starts with scanning the market for popular items, such as bestselling books. Then these are rewritten as a script, from which storyboards are created. The storyboards are shown to viewer panels in raw video form, to find out if the script has the potential to be a hit. On the basis of this test, it either goes into production for the cinema, or for television.

For example, *Despicable Me 1* and *2* became very successful animated films. It was discovered that the little yellow dolls that feature in the films—the *Minions*—were very popular. So, they decided to produce a series of four short TV episodes about the *Minions* to discover if these characters had a future of their own. The series proved very popular and, on this basis, it was decided to produce the film *Minions*. With revenues around $1.2 billion, *Minions* is one of the world's top 10 most successful films, generating more profit than *Despicable Me I* and *II* combined.

Even design-conservative Harley–Davidson does not shy away from experimentation. Around 1980, the brand was on its last legs; then, partly due to the introduction of Lean, but also to a brilliant concept they created called the Harley Owners Group, the company emerged stronger from this crisis. Harley customers are notoriously addicted to the distinctive hard-roaring sound of the engines, yet Harley–Davidson dared to experiment with a silent electric motor: *Project Livewire*. By taking a prototype on a global tour, the company gathered feedback from thousands of motorcyclists.

Volvo also continues to experiment with its innovations. This is the company that invented the safety cage, the three-point seat belt, active head restraints, the child lock, wide-angle mirrors, the third brake light, the airbag, the crumple zone, automatic braking in a collision, pedestrian detection, and much more. Spending on research and development, as a percentage of gross domestic product, differs strongly per country. Japan tops the OECD list with 3.6 percent on average, followed by Scandinavian and German-speaking countries (around 3 percent). Italy, Ireland, and Canada are at the bottom of the list, spending about 1.4 percent, while the US is an average spender with approximately 2.6 percent.

In that context, it might be worth taking a look at the TED video, *The Marshmallow Challenge*—a fun experiment to do with your colleagues. Using twenty sticks of spaghetti, one meter of string, and a meter of tape, try to build the highest tower possible within eighteen minutes, finishing it with a marshmallow on top. Most teams do not manage to build something that remains standing. The least successful are MBA students and executive teams. And the most successful? Maybe painful to hear, but they are toddlers. Why? Instead of using valuable time considering the possibilities and devising a plan, they get straight to work. They just try out what does and does not work. This immediate "prototyping" quickly points the way to the highest structures. The only ones who can compete with the toddlers are architects. A comforting thought, isn't it?

4.2   Test Fast, Fail Fast, Adjust Fast

Have you heard of the *Fosbury Flop*? Here's a hint. It has nothing to do with failure. If you're an occasional watcher of athletics, then you'll know it for sure, but perhaps not consciously. It is the technique used by high jumpers. They approach the bar from the side, springing up backwards and curling their body over the bar, landing on their backs on the cushion.

Every high jumper does it this way, but only since 1968. Until then, the technique was either "diving" forward over the bar or using a scissor movement of the legs. Between 1953 and 1963, records were frequently broken until, in 1963, the sport hit a plateau. A year later, an American student, Dick Fosbury, found the conventional techniques too complicated for him. He was a mediocre athlete who had never won anything. He began to experiment and, after endless failures, he found, more or less by accident, the technique which made him famous. Initially, his teammates laughed at him, until suddenly one event after another he began to win, eventually taking gold at the 1968 Olympics. He examined what the competition was doing and then invented his own distinctive approach. It didn't take long for the competition to change to the new technique, so that from 1971 on jump heights increased rapidly. By the way, the current record dates back to 1993.

Because Fosbury dared to fail, he won prizes he would otherwise never have won. However, there appear to be even more advantages.

Lower Costs

There is also scientific evidence for the benefits of failure. This was demonstrated by professor Barry Boehm within the context of software development. In 1979, on the basis of empirical research, he came up with two concepts, now known as *Boehm's Law:*

1. Errors are most frequent during the requirements and design activities and become exponentially more expensive the later they are removed.

2. A prototyping approach significantly reduces the number of requirements and design errors.

Imagine this: you are working at NASA and responsible for the launch of the Mars Rover. This must follow a precise orbit around the Earth, then Venus, and then Mars where, after a year's journey, it must land safely. You make a mistake when setting the direction of the launcher, a tiny deviation of just one millimeter at the nose of the 50 meter-long rocket. That may not seem like much, just 0.001 degrees of a full 360 degree circle. But, for convenience sake, lets simplify the example and let the rocket fly in a straight line direct to Mars, a distance of about 50 million kilometers. With our starting deviation of one millimeter, our rocket will eventually pass by Mars at 1,000 kilometers distance. And correcting a deviation of 1,000 kilometers at the end is, for many reasons, rather more difficult than correcting for one millimeter at the start.

Boehm's advice is to make as many errors (or prevent them) as early as possible after the start of a process. This reduces the likelihood that you'll have to recover from much greater damage at a later stage. The cost of adapting to failure and prevention are at their lowest at the start of the process, so you will earn these back in multiples.

Success through failure; an interesting paradox.

Many Failures Led the Way

What the example of Dick Fosbury makes clear, is that experimentation can lead to discoveries and improvements. But that experimenting is inextricably linked with failure. Failures are part of the learning process. Abraham Lincoln said: "The person who is incapable of making a mistake, is incapable of anything", and Antony James Froude said: "Mistakes are often the best teachers." Making mistakes happens just as much these days. At one point, J. K. Rowling sat, feeling totally useless, after a raft of "book" failures. But, this appears to have been just what inspired her to write her first Harry Potter novel. And Walt Disney was once fired from a local newspaper because he "lacked imagination and had no good ideas." Oprah Winfrey, Jerry Seinfeld, and Elvis Presley overcame similar circumstances. The two founders of Home Depot, which is now worth $166 billion, were once fired together from a small DIY store. James Dyson needed 5,127 failed attempts before he realized his vision of a revolutionary vacuum cleaner. It earned him billions (and without doubt brought relief to his patient wife).

Worldwide, there is growing understanding of the value of failure, celebrated in *FuckUp Nights* and *Failcon* events. These are meetings and conferences where people talk about their own experiences of failure and the lessons they learned. It was with refreshing humor and self-ridicule that, two years ago, some scientists shared their fieldwork mistakes via Twitter (search for hashtag #FieldWorkFail). Some enlightened organizations even document their "failures" in their annual reports.[1] According to Google Ngram—which analyzes the frequency certain phrases occur in digital books, articles, blogs, and so on—around 1980 "learning from failure" occurred as often as "learning from success"; nowadays it occurs six times more often. Hopefully a sign, albeit faint, of a positive development.

Maybe it is best summed up by the failed baseball player, and most successful basketball player ever, Michael Jordan. "I've missed more than 9,000 shots in my career. I've lost almost 300 games. 26 times I've been trusted to take the winning shot, and missed. I've failed over and over and over again in my life. And that is why I succeed." And: "I can accept failure; everyone fails at something. But I can't accept not trying."

So, being unafraid to fail is key to becoming creative and successful, as we shall see below.

4.3   Fear of Failure Limits Creativity

Research by the international Hay Group, among over 18,000 employees in 2,200 companies,[2] indicates that failure is still rarely considered as a way to learn. The top 20 best-performing companies in this group were compared with the rest. This showed that 72 percent of the companies in the top 20 see failing (after a good attempt) as an opportunity to learn and not something to be ashamed of. For the other companies, the figure was 59 percent. Similar results are seen for making it possible to provide innovation or improvement ideas to management.

Research by the European Union, among workers and entrepreneurs between 18 and 35 years old, shows that 83 percent of them believe that failure is good for personal development and that 74 percent would give someone who has failed a second chance. At the same time, 50 percent believe that failure will generate a negative image of them and 62 percent would not expect to get a second chance after a failure.[3] According to Harvard research, executives estimate that only 2 percent to 5 percent of the failures in their organizations are actually blameworthy, but that in 70 percent to 90 percent of failures someone is considered culpable.[4] Not surprisingly, many people deny failure, or blame others or circumstances.

In Europe, entrepreneurs whose businesses have gone bankrupt are often seen as failures and have difficulty getting funding for a new company, while similar entrepreneurs in the United States find it much easier to get a second chance.[5]

The key is to make a clear distinction between the preparation and execution of an experiment and its results. Leaders should demand top quality in the first, but be aware this can still generate a disappointing result. So encourage "outside-the-box" thinking, cherish people who color outside the lines, and reward people who look for desired paths.

The F-word: Away with the Social Taboo around Failure

For most companies, experimentation should be a major focus, because many successful improvements and innovations have emerged from pioneering entrepreneurship. It forms the basis for the policy that most *private equity* investors choose for start-ups: roughly speaking, for every ten investments at least nine fail or perform only moderately. It seems there is always one, which is wildly successful and recoups the total investment for all ten several times over. As Augustine said around 400 AD, "Si fallor, sum," which can translate as "I am because I make mistakes." A more-populist version was used by the cult figure Bob Ross, during his fascinating painting lessons on television. "We do not make mistakes, we just have happy little accidents."

Many scientists and researchers have achieved breakthroughs in the past by being willing and able to fail. Thomas Edison, the famous inventor and founder of General Electric, spent two years in his laboratory trying to make his light bulb. He said: "I have not failed. I've just found 10,000 ways that don't work," and "Genius is one per cent inspiration and 99 percent perspiration." Andre Geim felt his lab was a safe place to get things wrong, that there was room for error. He and his colleagues were allowed to spend 10 percent of their time on "silly things that might fail altogether." This took place on their "Friday Evenings" and led to the discovery of graphene, for which he later received the Nobel Prize.[6] Both NASA and Google stimulate spending work time on this kind of research; in Google, this is known as the *20 percent rule*. That this has brought Google many successful innovations is quite an understatement.

Accidental Discoveries

One of the nice things about daring to fail is that you can make disruptive discoveries completely outside your area of focus. For example, you discover, accidentally, that your client seems to attach great value to a feature of your product which you considered totally irrelevant. This is known as the *serendipity effect*. Unexpectedly, you find useful and valuable things while looking for something very different—a surprise bonus. US researcher Julius Comroe put it this way: "Serendipity is looking in a haystack for a needle and discovering a farmer's daughter." More reason to accept failure as something valuable. So have fun fiddling, playing around, experimenting, trying, and dabbling; the English have a wonderful word for this: *tinkering*.

Just take a look at the following concepts and products, and ask yourself what you think they have in common: a perfect round soccer ball; the world wide web; Google; Facebook; Viagra; Post-it Notes; cornflakes; dynamite; saccharine; the microwave oven; Velcro; Vaseline; Coca-Cola; penicillin; anesthesia; paperclips; the Slinky; Super Glue; Play-Doh; radioactivity; safety glass; potato chips/crisps; champagne; popsicle; teabags; sanitary napkins; chocolate-chip cookies;

vulcanization; chewing gum; inkjet printer; yo-yo; Frisbee; Listerine; glow-in-the-dark (phosphorus); X-rays; ice-cream cones; stainless steel; PTFE; matches; cellophane; plastic.

Does is ring a bell yet? These famous breakthroughs all happened by chance, by mistake or originally served a different purpose.[7] So, long live those who dared to experiment. The list is an ode to *accidental discovery.* Are you curious to find out more about these inventions in detail? Please go to mikehoogveld.com to read the full stories behind them, it is a really fascinating phenomenon.

Controlled Experimenting and Failing

These inventions show how chance can sometimes lend a hand. But wouldn't you find it great if, in your organization, you could use an approach where luck has an accepted role? A way of working where everyone focuses on continuous improvement and innovation by experimenting in smart and structured ways, where failure has a defined place? So your organization can adapt quickly to changing circumstances and lead the industry in innovation?

Yes? Then the next few chapters will certainly interest you. In Chapter 5, you can read about how agility is used in situations where winning is the only goal: warfare and sport. And in Chapter 6, you can delve into the history of agile management and its benefits. Then you'll see, in Chapter 7, what agile management is in concrete terms and precisely what it can mean for you and your organization.

By reading this chapter, you should now understand the following:
- *Failure is useful. According to Boehm's laws, this is best done as much and as early as possible in the process. Because the later you do it, the greater the cost.*
- *An additional advantage of failure is that it frequently leads to unexpected discoveries. This so-called serendipity has yielded many valuable inventions in various fields, such as the World Wide Web, Google, Facebook, Viagra, and Post-it Notes.*
- *Unfortunately, many organizations suffer from fear of failure, which unnecessarily limits their creativity and agility. Experimenting and trying-out is the watchword here.*

References

1. *Financieele Dagblad*, 19-12-2015.
2. Hay Group. (2014). *9th Annual Best Companies for Leadership Study.*
3. Think Young—Fail 2 Succeed. (2015). *Overcoming the Stigma of Failure.*
4. Edmondson, A. C. (2011). *Strategies for Learning from Failure.* Brighton: Harvard Business Review.
5. Ministry of Economy and Economic Bureau ING. (2001). *Financiers and Failed Entrepreneurs.*
6. Lewis, S. (2014). *The Rise.* New York: Simon and Schuster.
7. Various sources, including Wikipedia.

CHAPTER 5

When Winning is Necessary

There is nothing wrong with change, if it is in the right direction. To improve is to change; so to be perfect is to change often.

—Winston Churchill

By now, you'll have seen that organizations increasingly have to deal with changing circumstances and, therefore, adaptability is necessary in order to survive. Also, you'll have read that adaptability is not possible without the courage to experiment and fail. In this chapter, you can read how it can help in situations where winning is necessary.

5.1   A Turning Point in the History of the Modern World

As Winston Churchill, on May 10, 1940, took office as prime minister, the once mighty United Kingdom teeters on the edge of the abyss. After a dramatic First World War, its global empire is in decline and the treasury coffers are all but empty. British defences have been severely weakened; military equipment is outdated and organizational structures and strategies are unsuitable for modern warfare. At the same time, a very strong Nazi Germany is advancing decisively across both the European mainland and sea, leaving England completely isolated. Creative solutions are needed, and quickly.

Churchill realizes, immediately, that he has a huge challenge: "The Chiefs of Staff worked as a separate and almost independent body without direction or control by the Prime Minister [. . .]. Moreover, the leaders of the three armed forces had no shared view of the war as a whole. They were, unfortunately, far too influenced by the departmental vision of their individual armed forces."[1] Churchill directly introduces a new way of decision making, which is faster and more flexible: the defence committee. This meets daily and consists of the Deputy Prime Minister, the three Ministers of the Armed Forces, and the three Chiefs of Staff. This allows for a very fast process, where integrated planning is developed, executed, evaluated, and adjusted. In addition, Churchill personally directs a new department, *Combined Operations*, which coordinates cooperation between the navy, army, and air force at the operational level.

Churchill has no lack of ideas, work ethic, and inspiration (from, among others, Sun Tzu[27] and Von Clausewitz[28]). He employs a whole squadron of secretaries, available 24 hours a day, to record and distribute his dictations and notes. He is in a hurry, and rightly so. He firmly believes that finding the key to the solution of the war crisis is, as much as is possible in practice, in trying out new ideas. That there will also be a lot of not-so-good ideas that lead to failures, he accepts as a calculated risk. If something does not work, the plan will be adjusted immediately or abandoned. For Churchill top speed is, literally and figuratively, vital. He becomes notorious for his memos adorned with red stickers that demand: *"ACTION THIS DAY!"*

For his new approach, Churchill surrounds himself with numerous top scientists, such as mathematicians, physicists, chemists, biologists, astronomers, and engineers. He instructs them to work closely together to achieve the technological breakthroughs he considers essential to winning the war. Soon, this special research department becomes known, unofficially, as *Churchill's Toyshop* (the model for Department Q in the Bond novels of Ian Fleming). Along with many failures, the *Toyshop* delivers a raft of inventions that play an important role in the Allied victory, such as radar, tanks, amphibious landing craft, quick-build bridges, movable harbors, magnetic ship mines, time bombs, land mines, and portable antitank missiles.

Another creative group, consisting of economists, business administrators, and military strategists, are tasked with developing brand-new combat tactics. One such example is *Special Forces*: small fighting units, like paratroopers and commandos, who perform rapid interventions and are very maneuverable in the field. Or the *Special Operations Executive*, responsible for undercover operations. The creation of the Department of Economic Warfare is a powerful innovation. It weakens the enemy by economic sanctions and sabotage of the logistical supply lines for equipment, personnel, fuel, food, and currency.

In addition, Churchill sees the value of information and evaluation to continuously improve the British war effort. To this end, he founds a team with the somewhat strange name *Central Statistical Office*. Churchill wants complex problems described, as much as possible, in quantitative terms, to facilitate scenario analyses. Moreover, he does not trust the reports from the various defence units, and wants to gather all the statistical material within one common framework. On the other hand, he wants to outwit Germany and so he invests significantly in the British secret intelligence service. For example, he creates a secret team at Bletchley Park, with the aim of cracking German communications encryption which uses the Enigma code-machine. Under the leadership of Alan Turing and with much patience, the project is ultimately successful, and the Allies are able to translate all German communications without their knowledge. Not only does this shorten the war, but the machine translation engine they develop later becomes the basis of what we now know as the computer.

In short, Churchill transforms the British defence into an organization that works intensively together, is agile and fast, and freely experiments with innovations while analyzing feedback data to continuously improve its approach. This way of working, and of course the alliance that includes the US and Canada, results in a powerful force, and, towards the end of 1944, Germany can no longer resist. This, undoubtedly, was a turning point in modern history.

As a result, Churchill can be considered as one of the first individuals in history to create an "agile" organization. And, therefore, we must forgive him for inventing the "siren suit," the origin of the now infamous "onesie."

Twenty years later, someone else was also very successful at creating an "agile" organization, albeit in a completely different context.

5.2   Agility in Elite Sports

The person referred to above is Rinus Michels, to whom are attributed the famous words: "Football is war." (Bill Shankly put this in perspective by stating: "Some people believe football is a matter of life and death. I am very disappointed with that attitude. I can assure you it is much, much more important than that.") So, perhaps the step from war to sport is smaller than you think. You can investigate this idea further in the fields of football, baseball, and cycling.

Football

Rinus Michels is widely regarded as the person most responsible for the modern game by breaking with the classic English *Kick and Rush* tactics. Between 1965 and 1971, as coach of Ajax, he develops what comes to be known as "total football". This entirely new style of play, starting in a 4-3-3 formation, requires players to be able to change position constantly and take over each other's tasks as the game situation demands. Also, the players must always be available to receive the ball, in order to keep the passing-tempo high. It results in proactive tactics, aiming to win the ball in the opponent's half by allowing the opponent no time on the ball. Moreover, possession is maintained as long as possible, then sudden fast attacks are carried out. Therefore, intensive communication is needed between the coach and his captain, and between the captain and the rest of the team, to ensure players change position appropriately as the play changes.

This requires that players have excellent technique, are versatile, very fit, and have a good understanding of the game. This is developed by regular training using common game situations and working on players' flexibility, strength, speed, and endurance. There are now specialized coaches for every position. Michels also introduces competitive analysis. Before each game, he examines in detail the playing style of the opponents and then adjusts his tactics to negate and overcome them.

Ajax is extremely successful. Under Michels's leadership, Ajax top the Dutch league four times, win the Dutch Cup three times, and twice reach the European Cup Final. In 1971, Michels leaves to manage FC

Barcelona, where his approach, once again, brings success, winning the Spanish league and cup. In the World Cup year of 1974, Michels takes over the Dutch national team for four months, where he brings in total football. His approach takes the team, for the first time in history, to the World Cup Final. In 1986, he returns as national coach to begin qualification for the 1988 European Championships, which the Dutch team goes on to win. This was not a reason, even temporarily, for Michels to be less his sharp and observant self. After the Championships, during a celebratory boat ride through the Amsterdam canals, a football reporter says to him: "I see you got a new watch from the players. That must have been an emotional moment for you. "In his beautiful Amsterdam accent, Michels responds with: "*They* say it is new, so we'll just assume it is."

In 1988, after two very successful years as coach of Ajax, Johan Cruyff leaves for FC Barcelona. As Rinus Michels's "adept," he sees that the total football movement is slowly ebbing away and he decides to blow new life into it. In the following eight years, Barcelona win an impressive range of prizes: winning the national championship four times, the European Cup twice, the Super Cup four times, and the Spanish Cup once. Barcelona becomes the home and the "university" of total football, where, when Cruyff leaves, it is refined by Louis van Gaal, Frank Rijkaard, Pep Guardiola, and Luis Enrique into the world's most successful football system: "tiki-taka." The distinguishing factor of tiki-taka, besides superb technique of course, is speed of passing and movement.

Baseball

Around 2005, tiki-taka football takes on a new dimension; big clubs like FC Barcelona accelerate and increase their use of "intelligence." Aided by *video motion* systems and statistical analyses, games, tactics, players, and training are assessed for effectiveness. In addition, research is applied to the effectiveness of nutrition, the balance between work and rest, and between strength and endurance. All this results from the momentum achieved by the success of the Oakland Athletics baseball team. They are the first sports team in the world to apply the principles of *sabermetrics*. Attributed to coach Bill James, the approach collects objective data about baseball matches and players by statistically analyzing match activity.

In 1997, when Billy Beane is appointed general manager of the Oakland Athletics, he finds a team with very few prospects. For many years, they have been playing in the lower regions of Major League Baseball (MLB), from which you cannot be relegated. The facilities are outdated, the plays are all of only moderate ability, and the budget is the second lowest of the 30 MLB teams. Beane finds, too, that he has inherited a scouting and technical staff who are using very old-fashioned principles. Beane immediately hires an econometrist, who uses publicly available match statistics and a mathematical algorithm to analyze which players, in which positions, are most effective to win a match. This allows him to let costly and ineffective players go, and transfer-in very effective players, with low transfer fees and low salaries compared with other teams.

This means that the team can compete with top teams like the New York Yankees, who have three times the budget. In 2000, for the first time—in a very long time—the Oakland Athletics get in the divisional playoffs, and do so for four consecutive years. In 2006, they even reach the finals, the national playoffs. In 2002, they were the first team in the history of MLB to win twenty consecutive games.

Soon almost all MLB teams have adopted this approach, forcing Beane to be creative and expand his approach to other success factors. In 2012, this gets the Oakland Athletics into the playoffs again, and, in 2013, they repeat their 2006 performance, still with one of the lowest budgets in the sport. This success story is so remarkable that it is enshrined in a book that becomes very influential in baseball, *Money ball: The Art of Winning an Unfair Game*, by Michael Lewis, published in 2003. In 2011, it is made into a film.

But it's not just in baseball that something special happened; cycling also appears to be developing in a very interesting way.

Road Bicycle Racing

Which country do you think, in the last decade, has been the most successful in cycling? Most likely you'll think of France, Belgium, or Spain. Or perhaps Germany, Italy, or the United States. However, it is none of these countries, even though all have made a huge impression on this sport in the past. The honor goes to a (then) *dark horse* in the sport: Britain. Let's see how this happened.

WHEN WINNING IS NECESSARY   55

It's 2003. In the sports-mad UK, much of the population is frustrated, as the country still only plays a marginal role in many of the sports it invented, such as soccer, rugby, golf, cricket, tennis, hockey, and polo. British cycling could only hold fast to the Olympian concept that "The most important thing is not winning . . . but taking part". In this sport, the country has never been taken seriously. For a Brit, cycling is simply not second nature. Whenever someone dares to create an ambitious plan to bring British cycling to a higher level, it is invariably dismissed as a joke.

Yet, in 2003, someone appears on the scene who does not have these preconceptions. He answers to the name of Dave Brailsford. In 1997, while working as a sales manager at a bicycle importer, he gets into the British Cycling Federation, initially in an advisory role. Because he has a clear vision to improve athletic performance, six years later, he is made the *performance director*. And from that moment on, a small miracle unfolds.

His approach is as simple as it is effective. Brailsford believes in a philosophy he calls *Marginal Gains*. This is not just an idea; it is based on a sound mathematical concept: exponential growth. He approaches the sport of cycling as a process. He assumes that if he can realize incremental improvements of as little as 1 percent, in individual processes, they'll accumulate into a significant overall improvement. He needs the *maximum number of opportunities for improvement*, so he takes a holistic perspective. He not only looks at major factors such as diet, training, and equipment, but also secondary factors, which are overlooked by almost everyone else.

Here are just some of the "small" things he investigated:

- By analyzing the mechanics' area in the team truck, he discovered that dust was accumulating on the floor, which undermines bike maintenance. So, he orders the floor painted stark white, so that any contaminants stand out immediately.
- He makes sure that the riders are informed about hygiene and makes them use antibacterial hand gel to reduce infection. He also runs tests with different massage gels to find the most effective formulation.
- Each rider tries different pillows to find which gives him the best night's sleep. He uses the pillow at home, but it also travels with him to training camps and hotels.

- He researches the relationship between the intensity of cooldown and speed of recovery. One popular measure he takes is to make the team bus more comfortable, promoting faster recovery.
- During wind tunnel experiments, he notes that the race bikes are not as aerodynamic as they could be. Therefore, he oversees adjustments to the frame, wheels, pedals, and handlebars.

In short, he leaves nothing to chance and is looking always and everywhere for things to improve. He unravels all the processes down to their smallest components and searches for latent problems and incorrect assumptions. In addition, he sees faults and weaknesses not as a threat, but as an opportunity to make adjustments and to realize marginal gains. Because the changes are mostly small, usually they can be achieved quickly, bringing almost immediate results as a consequence.

Was any of this worth it? The results, under Brailsford's leadership, speak for themselves. In 2004, Britain won two cycling gold medals at the Olympic Games, the best British performance since 1908. In 2008, 2012, and 2016, Britain dominates and wins the most cycling medals of all countries: 38 in total. Of these, 22 are gold, 36 percent of the possible gold medals. In that same period, British cyclists won 83 world championships. Based on his success, in 2010 Brailsford is asked to become manager of a newly established British professional cycling team, Team Sky. No British team has ever won the Tour de France and the aim is to achieve this within five years. It happens much faster than that. Led by Brailsford, first Bradley Wiggins and then Chris Froome take the yellow jersey in 2012, 2013, 2015, 2016, and in 2017. In 2009, Brailsford is honored for his contribution to British sport, receiving the CBE from Queen Elizabeth; in 2013 he was knighted.

The Winner of Tomorrow

Examples from warfare and sport show how agility can help you when winning is necessary. And so to ensure that your organization is the winner in tomorrow's market. In the next chapter, you can read how agility-thinking has emerged, so you can better understand the procedures explained in the following chapters and their relevance to the agility of your organization.

In this chapter, you learned the following:

- *Agility is a crucial success factor for those who want to win. Practical examples from warfare and professional sports (football, baseball, and cycling) confirm this.*
- *To make yours a winning organization, it could be useful to apply insight from warfare and professional sports.*

Reference

1. Best G. (2014). *Churchill*. Media peat.

CHAPTER 6

Agility

Being Fast and Responsive

*It is better to act quickly and err than to hesitate until
the time of action is past.*
—Carl Von Clausewitz

In the previous chapter, you read about the need to win and the role
agility plays in it. This chapter continues the discussion. You'll see
how agility-thinking has evolved historically and discover why agility is
necessary in your organization also.

6.1 The Emergence of Agile Management from Twelve Ideas

In agile management, continuous adjustment and improvement are
central. Of course, this way of working didn't just fall from the sky. Agile
management has a long history, based on twelve ideas, which are briefly
shown below as a time line in Figure 6.1.

Idea 1: The Scientific Method

Agility-thinking can actually be traced back to 1620, when Francis
Bacon—strongly influenced by his contemporary Galileo—puts the
scientific method down on paper. The concept is refined, between

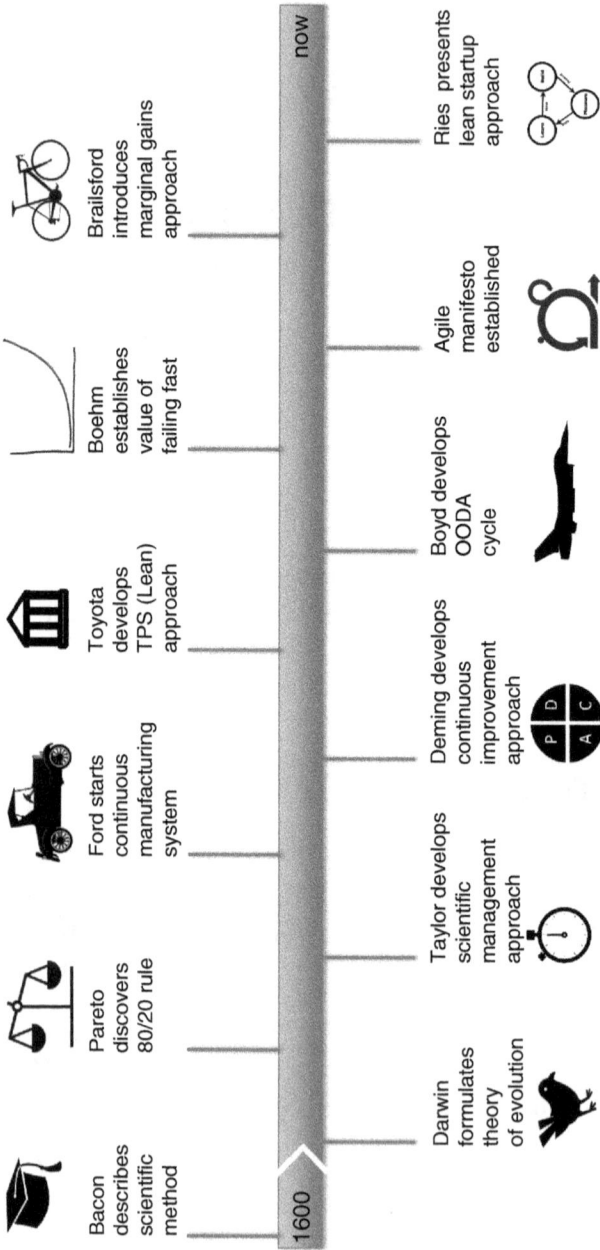

Bacon describes scientific method

Pareto discovers 80/20 rule

Ford starts continuous manufacturing system

Toyota develops TPS (Lean) approach

Boehm establishes value of failing fast

Brailsford introduces marginal gains approach

now

1600

Darwin formulates theory of evolution

Taylor develops scientific management approach

Deming develops continuous improvement approach

Boyd develops OODA cycle

Agile manifesto established

Ries presents lean startup approach

Figure 6.1 The historical development of agility-thinking

1870 and 1930, by Pierce, James, Lewis, and Dewy, whose approaches of Pragmatism and Empiricism[1] eventually merge into the, now well-established, Empirical Cycle[2]. In short, the scientific method sets down an iterative cycle of specific activities to develop knowledge. This cycle can be repeated infinitely to deepen understanding. The fixed steps within the cycle are:

- *Observation*: You do the process and see what happens.
- *Induction*: Based on your observations, you develop a general theory to explain them.
- *Deduction*: You translate this general theory to predictions, in the form of specifically formulated, testable hypotheses.
- *Testing*: You run an experiment to test your hypothesis.
- *Evaluation*: You evaluate the results of your experiment and, based on these, confirm or reject your hypotheses (also called *verification* and *falsification*).

After each iteration of the cycle is completed, you will have gained more insight into your question. This insight becomes the starting point for a new iteration. And so it continues.

This method is still standard in science, and as you will see it is also used, in a modified form, in business.

Idea 2: Darwinism

The influence on contemporary management theory of Darwin's vision of adaptivity cannot be overestimated. We discussed this in detail in Chapter 2.

Idea 3: The 80/20 Rule

It is not a boring year, 1848. It sees France, the Netherlands, Belgium, and the German, Italian, and Habsburg countries experiencing huge popular uprisings. In the history books, it becomes known as the "Revolution Year." It can hardly be a coincidence that precisely in that year, late in his life, someone in the world is making a revolutionary discovery.

Born in Paris, to an exiled Genoese marquis called Pareto and his French wife who, inspired by the German revolution, call their son Fritz Wilfred. Ten years later, the family returns to Italy and his parents decide to change his name to Vilfredo Federico. Vilfredo appears very eager to learn and, at just 21, he earns his doctorate in engineering. He starts work as a civil engineer for the Italian railway and moves on to manage several metal factories. He is politically very active, has a sharp pen, and is a feared opponent in duels with sword or pistol.

Around forty, after the death of his parents, he changes course radically. He quits his job, marries a Russian (who unfortunately leaves him in 1902 and takes up with their young servant) and moves to Switzerland. His academic curiosity begins to bubble up again, this time focused on economics and sociology. This leads to a professorship in Lausanne, where his research is increasingly focused on the distribution of money and political power. Many of his ideas are later used by his best student, in his own political career. This student just happens to be called Benito Mussolini.

In 1906, Vilfredo publishes some remarkable research. He finds that in Italy 80 percent of the assets are owned by 20 percent of the population. He concludes that this population, thereby, actually holds all the power and decides to call this group by the term "elite."

Apparently reassured by this insight, he decides that it is the time to let his lifestyle reflect his own wealth. He finds a new wife, buys a huge villa—which he fills completely with the most expensive art—assembles one of the largest wine and spirits collections in Europe and surrounds himself, for no apparent reason, with a huge number of Angora cats. He devotes himself in his final, elitist, years to mathematics, beauty, and pleasure. He dies in 1923, childless.

Pareto's name actually became particularly well known thanks to an American management consultant, Joseph Juran. In 1941, Juran encounters Pareto's work and decides to apply it to the issue of quality. He discovers that the 80/20 ratio applies to many different managerial phenomena and renames it the *Pareto Principle*. It becomes widely known as Pareto's Law, the 80/20 rule, the rule of the "Vital Few and Trivial Many," the Law of Imbalance and the Principle of Least Resistance (a derivative application developed by George Kingsley Zipf).

In general, the 80/20 rule means that 80 percent of the effect is caused by 20 percent of the input. This is not an empirically proven rule, but you can see it often and easily. The two numbers may also have a different relationship and not necessarily add up to 100. There may also be a ratio of 90–30, 70–40, and 50–5 (the latter means that, for example, there is a high amount of ineffective activity), but 80–20 will be by far the most common.

Some practical examples:

- 80 percent of profits come from 20 percent of customers
- 80 percent of pop music can be played using 20 percent of the chords
- 80 percent of sales in a restaurant come from 20 percent of the menu items
- 80 percent of data bandwidth is allocated to 20 percent of users
- 80 percent of users use 20 percent of software functionality
- 80 percent of complaints come from 20 percent of customers
- 80 percent of time spent in a supermarket involves 20 percent of the shopping
- 80 percent of traffic accidents are caused by 20 percent of road users
- 80 percent of downloaded music comes from 20 percent of performers
- 80 percent of cost is caused by 20 percent of the production process.

What does this mean now for agile management? First of all, the 80/20 rule forms the basis for the so-called *minimum viable product* (which is discussed further in Chapter 11). Here you strive to offer a proposition, at a minimal investment, which gives the customer an acceptable picture of the final product or service. So here you want to focus on the 20 percent of the functions that deliver 80 percent of his experience.

Secondly, logic says that, based on the 80/20 rule, time-use can also have an optimal point, and that benefit from additional time-use decreases rapidly. You can continue to analyze infinitely, because it can never be complete, but this leads to *analysis paralysis. Or worse, to death by analysis:* if you're not careful every initiative or idea is rejected on the basis of analysis. You have to dare to accept that your analysis, at a given moment, is complete enough, that you have spent enough time on it and that it is good enough. You just need to start somewhere, to dare to push the boat out. This touches a bit on Parkinson's Law, which states that work expands to fill the time available to do it. You can prevent this by setting time limits and sticking to them.

Thirdly, the 80/20 rule forms the basis for prioritization of development and improvement projects. If you invest in such projects, investment yield decreases rapidly as you move away from the 80/20 point. The always-scarce resources of time and money should be used with optimum efficiency, focusing on the factors that have maximum impact on the result. This requires managing different criteria, as you can read in chapter 10.

In addition to the above, there are a pair of unusual aspects of the 80/20 rule. The first is the *self-fulfilling prophecy*, defined by sociologist Robert Merton, in 1948, as follows:

"The *self-fulfilling prophecy* begins with a false definition of the situation, which evokes a new behavior that confirms the original false definition as true. The apparent accuracy of the prediction maintains a false misrepresentation of the situation. The predictor will point to what eventually happened as evidence that he was correct at the beginning."

The economy is a prime example, where media coverage about a faltering economy greatly contributes to the start of economic decline, or leads to predictions of a rise in stock prices, which actually cause the increase. Google searches are a good example of how it manifests in marketing and sales; the top 3 results commanding circa 63 percent of the click-throughs. Due to this popularity, they return, in subsequent searches, again in the top 3, and so on. The principle applies to all kinds of popularity rankings (such as the music Top 40), leading to the phenomenon whereby if something has been judged as popular, it will continue to be seen as such and perhaps become even more popular. A self-maintaining system. Probably, in your organization, the best-selling products or services get the most attention and the biggest communications budget, because in general businesses focus more on short rather than long-term sales. Obviously, this carries the risk that the full potential of existing or new products and services is unlikely ever to be realized, as they never get a chance to prove themselves. It is important to be aware of this.

The second special unusual aspect of the 80/20 rule is that of the *long tail,* a mathematical concept which became famous after Chris Anderson's 2004 article in *Wired* magazine.[3] In statistics, a *long tail* (or *fat-tail*) means that a larger proportion of the population rests within the long tail of a probability distribution than in a normal distribution. Companies like Spotify, iTunes, Netflix, and Amazon are taking full advantage of this. Due to low marginal costs, and the transparency caused by good search capabilities, they can offer a huge amount of online "niche"-content and products. When added together, this realizes more than half their income. So, this is actually a clever reverse application of the 80/20 rule. As an Amazon employee so aptly put it: "Today we sell more books that weren't selling well yesterday, than books that were flying off the shelves yesterday." Hooray for the lost souls of slow-moving inventory.

Idea 4: Scientific Management

Around 1900, an important part of the scientific method is first applied within companies: Frederick Taylor, the founder of scientific management, introduces a way of doing business which aims to achieve performance improvements based on detailed analyses. Decisions should be made on purely rational grounds; central to this philosophy is measuring performance and comparing the results to objective standards. Taylor's vision is supported, among others, by Frank Bunker Gilbreth. He is a pioneer in using time and method studies to improve performance, for which he develops the now widely used visual approach of *process flow mapping.*

Idea 5: Continuous Manufacturing

Taylorism and the time and method study approach are picked up by Henry Ford. In 1903, following two bankruptcies, the carmaker founds the Ford Motor Company and is quite successful with his Model A. It's now 1908 and a new era is dawning. Until then, owning a car was reserved only for the rich, but Ford decides to make the car accessible to the masses and introduces the Model T Ford. This becomes very successful when, in 1910, he moves the Ford factory to a new place where he has the space to realize his brilliant creation: the assembly line. It is the first in history.

His continuous-production line greatly shortens assembly times for the Model T, allowing him to dramatically reduce the price from $950 to $680 dollars (the assembly line was also "responsible" for the famous quote, "A customer can have a car painted any color that he wants, so long as it's black," as this was the only paint available that dried fast enough for the new production speed). Ford knows how to continuously optimize his manufacturing processes, giving him a decades-long cost advantage over the competition. During World War II, the United States war effort benefits tremendously from this process, quickly scaling-up production of ammunition, weapons, and equipment to previously unimaginable levels.

Idea 6: The PDCA Cycle

The same US government sends the professor and statistician W. Edwards Deming, in 1950, to Japan as a quality-management advisor to help with the country's postwar reconstruction. Deming's premise is that improving quality leads to a reduction in spending and an increase in productivity and market share. His work is inspired by the physicist Walter Shewhart who, in 1939, developed the first fully scientific approach to process improvement. The Shewhart Cycle has three distinct steps: *specification, production,* and *inspection*. While in Japan, Deming develops this into what we now know as the *Plan–Do–Check–Act* cycle (PDCA) or the *Deming Wheel*. The cycle now has four steps, as follows:

1. *Plan*: Establishing improvement goals and the processes to achieve them.
2. *Do*: Implementing processes and measuring the output and results.
3. *Check*: Comparing the actual and expected results, and looking for discrepancies between planned and actual implementation of the processes.
4. *Act*: On the basis of insight gained, determining whether the approach outlined in the Plan-phase was an improvement over the previous approach (aka the standard or *baseline*). If so, then this becomes the new standard; if not, then the current baseline is kept. In both cases, there is still something to learn, which means that you can start a new iteration of the PDCA cycle.

A unique feature of the PDCA cycle is that it can facilitate both major breakthroughs and frequent small improvements. Deming was convinced that what is not measured is not managed, let alone able be improved. He was always seeking a factual basis for decisions. His motto was: "In God we trust; all others bring data."

Idea 7: Toyota Production System (Lean)

What country, in your opinion, produces the best-quality cars overall? Chances are your first thought is Germany. Understandable, with all those expensive premium brands like BMW, Audi, and Mercedes. But it is Japan. Every year, organizations such as the Consumers' Association, the Dutch ANWB, British AA and RAC, and the USA's AAA compile data on millions of cars, to establish their monthly costs for maintenance and repair, and then compare these costs with the list price, age of the car, and the mileage. This totally objective scoring system has, for many years, shown that Japanese brands such as Honda, Nissan, and Mazda are by far the best. Toyota even stands head and shoulders above the other Japanese brands.

Toyota Motor Corporation is founded just before the Second World War, but struggles well into the fifties with the problem that weak homeland demand forces them to produce many different models in small numbers. The successful American production approach originated by Ford, focusing on large numbers and efficiency, isn't applicable: Toyota needs a highly flexible production system. At the same time, founder Kiichiro Toyoda's vision is to build the best cars in the world. His production chief Taiichi Ohno is inspired by the way American supermarkets allow customers to pick the products they want from the shelves and then, based on the quantities sold, buy new stock. Together, Toyoda and Ohno develop a management philosophy that focuses on creating value by achieving the lowest cost, highest quality, and shortest lead times. Central to this is *kaizen*, a continuous-improvement approach based on Deming's PDCA cycle. Around this core, they create a profound culture, which makes use of a very large set of instruments such as *teamwork*, *waste reduction*, *just-in-time*, and *jidoka* (quality control).[4] They cleverly structure the daily work of managers and employees around these methods, so that they are constantly making small improvements in their work processes. Although this costs little time and effort, the long-term cumulative benefits are considerable.

This makes Toyota very successful, yet the company is modest about its achievements. Eventually, it grows into the largest car manufacturer in the world, with the highest brand value and, as we've already seen, the highest quality.

Their success, of course, did not go unnoticed by western car manufacturers. In the early eighties, the Toyota Production System is translated into a western approach, known as *Lean*. The success of Lean sees it applied in the production processes of other sectors and, gradually, it finds its way into the "soft" sectors such as *services*.[5]

Idea 8: OODA Cycle

We've seen, from the Churchill story, that agile management learned valuable insights from warfare. In the seventies and eighties, we see something similar occurring in the US military, in the person of John Boyd. Boyd was an Air Force pilot who, around the fifties, flew missions in Korea. After his active service, he was appointed head of the education section of the USAF Weapons School, for which he authors its tactical manuals. Soon he gets the nickname *Forty Second Boyd* because he dares to bet every fighter pilot that, as their instructor and starting at a disadvantage, he can beat every opponent within forty seconds.

Over the years, he becomes fascinated by the theories behind *air-to-air* tactics. He is so passionate that his nickname slowly changes to the *Mad Major* (other nicknames circulating are *Genghis John*—because of his confrontational style of debate—and the *Ghetto Colonel* because of his spartan lifestyle.) We can assume he wasn't boring. Boyd immerses himself over a long period in military history: he examines guerrilla warfare and Hitler's blitzkrieg; the tactics of Clausewitz and the Romans, and even goes as far back as the 6th Century BC to Sun Tzu. He studies philosophy, history, and science and what we now know as chaos and complexity theory. He also develops mathematical models for simulating combat situations and is able predict the results of alternative tactics. On this basis, he formulates his *energy-maneuverability* theory.

His outspoken nature has made him many enemies in his immediate vicinity (most instructors in the elite Top Gun program, for example, would have been happy to see him dead.) However, successive US Secretaries of Defence are impressed by his theories, in particular for the development of new combat jets. Boyd makes a transition to the ministry and his theories are the basis for the new F-16 fighter. In the early nineties, he is even the architect behind the plans for Operation Desert Storm in Iraq.

But what vision was the foundation for his theories? On the basis of all his study, Boyd concluded that the key to victory lies in the ability to create situations in which a person or organization can make and execute the right decisions faster than the enemy. So everything revolves around responsiveness and speed of decision-making. The fastest pilot will win because his opponent is responding to a situation that has already changed. In the case of the F-16, Boyd wanted to build a fast, short, highly maneuverable combat fighter with superb all-round visibility from the cockpit, and quick-to-read instruments. To this end, he develops an aircraft that is very light, has a flexible and responsive engine, and is also the first to provide graphical cockpit-displays, *fly-by-wire* operation, and a canopy without metal frames offering seamless vision.

All this allows the pilot to continuously apply Boyd's OODA decision-making loop with maximum speed and quality. Boyd argues that all intelligent organisms and organizations undergo a continuous process of interaction with their environment. He describes this on the basis of four connected and overlapping steps, each passing seamlessly into the next

1. *Observation*: Data collection through the senses.
2. *Orientation*: The synthesis and analysis of data in order to form the current mental perspective.
3. *Decision*: Choosing an approach from the current mental perspective.
4. *Action*: The output of the approach.

Boyd's position was that this cycle is central to adaptivity and is crucial for survival and, in this case, in a much shorter timescale than Darwin thought. He believed that organizations such as companies or governments should have a hierarchy of OODA cycles: strategic, tactical, and operational. This would necessitate an optimally decentralized decision-making structure, one based on goal-oriented commands rather than action-driven (*achieve this*, in place of *do this*), to maximize the intellectual capacity and creative ability of employees. The latter is also known as *Power to the Edge* and aims to dynamically synchronize operations within organizations, in order to achieve maximum agility and optimize decision-making processes in a network organizational structure.

To achieve organizational goals, Boyd also suggested a combination of four main success factors: variation, speed, harmony, and initiative. He meant the following:

- *Variation*: The flexibility to easily switch from one operation to another, or to perform multiple actions simultaneously if necessary.
- *Speed*: The ability to respond quickly and to increase or decrease this speed as needed.
- *Harmony*: The competence to allow actions appropriate to the circumstances, and speed of developments, so that these actions positively influence each other in their development (*co-evolve*).
- *Initiative*: The willingness to assume leadership and take action to identify problems at the right time and resolve them.[6]

In short, Boyd's insights are fundamental to achieving agility.

Idea 9: The Spiral Model

In 1986 and 1988, Professor Barry Boehm publishes two papers which have a huge impact on the future of software development. As we saw in section 3.1, Boehm had discovered that it is most effective, in the development process, to make as many errors as possible (or to prevent them), as often as possible, and as early as possible, after the start of the process. This minimizes the need to fix problems at a later time, so the total failure, prevention, and repair costs are kept to a minimum. Boehm notes that the traditional waterfall method in which prolonged, static phases of design, construction, and testing occur individually and chronologically does not deliver optimal efficiency.

In order to put his insight into practice, he develops his *Spiral Model*, which he presents in an academic paper. Central to his model is an iterative process of prototyping, consisting of four steps:

1. Setting goals
2. Identifying and eliminating risks
3. Developing and testing
4. Planning the next iteration.

Via these four iterative steps, the prototype and related activities are refined until the final version of the software can de detailed and implemented. Boehm assumes, therefore, that certain important conditions are fulfilled. First, there must be enough time for all the iterations to complete. He also attaches great importance to the *requirements*. These must be agreed in advance and meet the expectations of the customer, after which they should change minimally, if at all. Additionally, the developers must have a common picture of the architecture that will meet the requirements. In essence, all of this comes together in the idea that the software must be developed and delivered in the smallest functioning parts possible.

In the decade after the launch of Boehm's approach, software development will change fundamentally. This approach is, therefore, also another foundation stone for future *agile development*.

Idea 10: Agile Development

In a meeting in 2001, a group of seventeen software developers, calling themselves the *Agile Alliance*, create a manifesto based on ideas that have been around since the late nineties. These ideas are a reaction to the traditional "waterfall" or "cascade" methods, which developers experience as bureaucratic, slow, ineffective, and hindering creativity. The manifesto covers several agile movements such as Scrum, Kanban, Extreme Programming, Adaptive Software Development, Dynamic Systems Development Method, Crystal, Feature-Driven Development, Pragmatic Programming, and Lean Software Development.

The purpose of the group is to create a development process that can adapt quickly to changing realities, such as the wishes of a client. In addition, the aim is to deliver software in the smallest possible working parts, so that it can be quickly tested, improved, and extended. In this iterative, incremental, and adaptive way of working, we can see a very short-cycle variation of the PDCA learning process. The *Manifesto for Agile Software Development* 2001[7] defines four values: that developers "prefer individuals and interactions over processes and tools, working software over comprehensive documentation, customer collaboration over contract negotiation, and responding to change over following a plan".

On the basis of these four values, the developers also formulate a dozen principles that they want to apply in practice.

1. The highest priority is to satisfy the customer through early and continuous delivery of valuable software.
2. Welcome changing requirements, even late in development. Agile processes harness change for the customer's competitive advantage.
3. Deliver working software frequently, from a couple of weeks to a couple of months, with a preference for the shorter timescale.
4. Business people and developers must work together daily throughout the project.
5. Build projects around motivated individuals. Give them the environment and support they need, and trust them to get the job done.
6. The most efficient and effective method of conveying information to and within a development team is face-to-face conversation.
7. Working software is the primary measure of progress.
8. Agile processes promote sustainable development. The sponsors, developers, and users should be able to maintain a constant pace indefinitely.
9. Continuous attention to technical excellence and good design enhances agility.
10. Simplicity—the art of maximizing the amount of work **not** done—is essential.
11. The best architectures, requirements, and designs emerge from self-organizing teams.
12. At regular intervals, the team reflects on how to become more effective, then tunes and adjusts its behavior accordingly.

Agile software development, and especially Scrum, has taken off and is now increasingly used, for example, in engineering, innovation, and marketing (there is even an agile marketing manifesto[8]). It also constitutes the most important pillar of the Lean Startup methodology.

Idea 11: Marginal Gains

In Section 5.2, we discussed the spectacular results Brailsford managed to achieve in British cycling with his "marginal gains" approach. This case shows the power of an investigative mentality combined with striving for continuous improvement. Many are convinced that change is only worthwhile if it results in a large, visible outcome, but Brailsford's approach proves otherwise.

The crux of continuous improvement lies in the fact that if you make improvements in a process, the results do not simply add up, they multiply (this effect is called "potentiation"). And this occurs in three ways:

1. Within the actual improvement, through infinite iterations.
   For example, in aviation, the thickness of the paint on the fuselage and wings has been gradually reduced, making the aircraft lighter and therefore more fuel efficient.
2. Interaction between the improvements, because improvement in one part can lead to an improvement within another part (or process).
   Example: by developing more-economical engines, the aircraft needs to carry less fuel. This makes the aircraft lighter and, again, more economical, so that it needs to carry less fuel and so on.
3. Combining improvements.
   Example: by flying the lighter aircraft a little slower, fuel economy is improved.

Through these effects, rapid, small changes cause a large multiplication in improvements. Figure 6.2 shows how this leads to an exponentially-increasing accumulative result.

The top line in Figure 6.2 is based on improvement steps of 1 percent and, after 200 iterations/ factors/interactions, leads to an improvement of 632 percent (increasing the steps to just 2 percent, for example, massively accelerates improvement to 5,148 percent). Although 200 iterations might seem high, experience has shown that a large number of multiplications can be achieved very quickly.

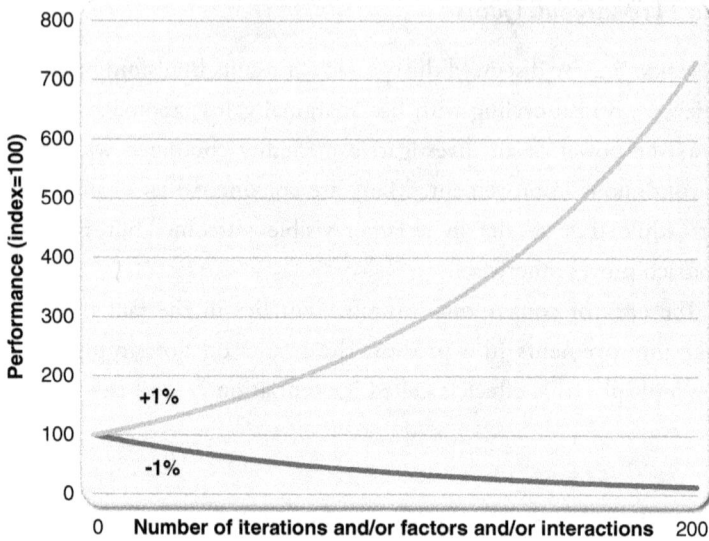

Figure 6.2 Repetition or combination of small improvements, resulting in strong growth performance

Idea 12: Lean Startup

Lean Startup is a method for setting up new companies, presented in 2011 for the first time, by Eric Ries.[9] Ries's method combines two approaches: the first is agile development, for rapidly developing workable online concepts; the second is the *customer discovery and validation* approach of Steve Blank, where identifying customer needs and creating propositions that meet them are central. Blank's approach is, in turn, largely based on the scientific method, which is used to test propositions with (potential) customers. Within Lean Startup, the PDCA cycle is again central, albeit in a slightly modified form. Ries calls this "validated learning" and therein uses the three steps of *building, measuring,* and *learning.* Just as in PDCA this is a continuous, iterative process, based on testing hypotheses and measuring the results in order to continue improving the propositions and the underlying business model.

The Lean Startup methodology has become very popular among technology start-ups in Silicon Valley and even has an international movement of discussion forums and events. Although Lean Startup focuses on online business, with some modifications, the method is also applicable to offline channels and tangible products. Even within governments, the method is being used successfully.

6.2   The Benefits of Agile Management

This short history shows that agile management is a way of working based on sound scientific evidence, wherein logic, experimentation, and measurement are crucial factors. Also, implementing agile management usually generates a sound business case. Unfortunately, at this time, the only "agile" studies published are in the context of software development. While one cannot simply project these onto wider applications of agile management, they do give an indication. The annual survey by Version One[10] shows that organizations implementing Agile derived the following benefits:

- 87 percent adapted better to changing priorities
- 84 percent saw higher team productivity
- 79 percent observed higher team motivation
- 78 percent noted higher work quality
- 77 percent realized shorter time-to-market
- 75 percent saw better alignment between IT and business.

Based on various studies on the deployment of agile, experts assume that the ratio of investment to outcome is, at the very least, 1:10, and that this result is not only achieved at the end of the deployment, but gradually, right from the start. In addition to the advantages listed above, organizations also benefit from greater agility, higher added value, better predictability and control over results, and increased customer satisfaction. It is not about efficiency, but about efficacy: the flow-speed in the value chain. Value flow, delivery speed, and customer satisfaction are also important indicators for measuring your organization's agility.[11]

Now that you understand the origins of agility and what it can deliver, it is high time we defined exactly what agile *management* is and what it is not. This is the subject of Chapter 7.

By reading this chapter, you'll have discovered the following:
- *Agility is important for organizations that want to perform optimally in the future. Toyota's huge success is a very clear example.*
- *Agile management is not a hype that has rapidly emerged and will disappear just as rapidly. It is based on principles from four centuries*

ago and has been refined from many different perspectives. It is, therefore, firmly grounded in science and practice.

- *Research in the context of IT strongly suggests that implementing agile management will yield a high return on investment.*

References

1. Moen, R., and C. Norman. (1990). *Evolution of the PDCA Cycle.*
2. de Groot, A. D. (1994). *Methodology; Foundations of Research and Thinking in the Behavioral Sciences.* Assen: Van Gorcum.
3. Anderson, C. (2004). "The Long Tail." *Wired Magazine.*
4. Liker, J. K. (2004). *The Toyota Way.* New York: McGraw-Hill.
5. Womack, J. P., and D. T. Jones. (2003). *Lean Thinking.* London: Simon & Schuster.
6. Hammond, G. T. (2012). *On the Making of History: John Boyd. The Harmon Memorial lecture.* US Air Force Academy.
7. See agilemanifesto.org
8. See agilemarketingmanifesto.org
9. Ries, E. (2011). *The Lean Startup.* New York: Crown Publishing.
10. Version One. (2014). *9th Annual State of Agile Survey.* Version One.
11. Solingen, R., and R. van Lanen. (2013). *Scrum for Managers.* Academic Service.

CHAPTER 7

The Essence of Agile Management

The only way to win is to learn faster than anyone else.

—Eric Ries

Based on the previous chapters we now know the relevance of agile management and its genesis. In this chapter we define what agile management is and on what principles agile management should be based.

7.1 Agile Management as an Integrated Approach

As you already saw in section 3.1, higher levels of VUCA (the volatility, uncertainty, complexity, and ambiguity of markets) require similar levels of agility. And because the VUCA level appears to be on the rise in most sectors, achieving agility should be relevant to most organizations. This applies equally to public authorities, nonprofit organizations, and commercial enterprises. As Gary Hamel once put it: "The only reliable advantage is a superior capacity to reinvent your business model *before* circumstances force you to do so."[1] No surprise then, that Jack Welch, the famous CEO of General Electric between 1981 and 2001, had the motto: "Change before you have to."

General Electric

Let us remain, for a moment, with the example of General Electric (GE). Like many companies, in the early nineties GE decides to transfer production to low-wage countries, in their case predominantly China. Between 2000 and 2012, however, wages increase by a factor of five. At the same time, the price of oil goes up by three times, significantly increasing transportation costs. This fundamentally changes the business case for offshoring. The problem is that GE no longer have the necessary knowledge and experience to go back to building its own products, this expertise is now the domain of its foreign contractors.

But in 2012, GE turns this disadvantage into an advantage: the company can start with a clean slate to design new production processes. Close by the head office, GE opens a small factory making refrigerators and stoves and employs new engineers and production workers. They discover that these products can be offered for a retail price that is approximately 20 percent lower than the Chinese versions. The success factor appears to be that GE's production workers now operate in an open, collegial and self-critical environment working directly with designers, engineers, marketers, and others in the production chain.

Even more important than cost reductions is the shortening of the product development cycle. This is made possible by having production and other functions work together in the same physical place. Shortening this cycle is necessary in order to keep up with the accelerating pace of product innovation, as household products no longer have a market lifetime of seven years, but just two or three. As a result, the plant has become a laboratory for innovation, which is able to adapt itself to changing customer needs and competitive environments.

Delivery times also come down significantly: instead of the five-week transit time from the Chinese factory to retailers in the United States, it is now one day (and even just thirty minutes to local stores). This enables GE to react quickly and adapt to changes in customer demand and production. Thus, GE massively reduces inventory costs. Also, they now rarely need to discount models that have become obsolete as a result of competitors bringing new and improved models to market. Very tangible results from agility.[2]

McDonald's

Something similar is happening at McDonald's. As a global fast-food brand serving 68 million customers daily, this organization is always under the critical lens of public opinion. Since its founding, in 1940, it has had to adapt regularly to changing requirements often brought about by changes in social perceptions. They have had to respond to paradigm shifts in issues such as health, nutrition, animal welfare, the environment, and working conditions. In the past decade, for example, a clear trend emerged as a demand for healthy food and quality coffee. Good espresso made Starbucks into a major new competitor for McDonald's.

As McDonald's notices that these developments are becoming more frequent and occurring faster, it is just a small step up from their lean way of working to move to agile management. Via frequent experimentation, McDonald's is able to accelerate renewal of its restaurants and products. It applies a process cycle of *try–listen–refine*. New ideas are tried small; if something does not work, McDonald's stops immediately, and if something is a success, they roll it out to all their restaurants as quickly as possible.

A concrete example is the use of touch screens to place and pay for orders. Or pilots for products or processes that occur in selected branches. In some stores, they tested allowing people to create their own burger. And in certain branches, they investigated how customers respond to concepts such as the McCafé and the Salad Bar. In still other restaurants, they've experimented with table service, or expanding the breakfast range. This encourages the perception that McDonald's is stronger than the competition in customer choice and experience. It continues to innovate, currently by testing smartphone ordering and payment. It's clear McDonald's values and prioritizes agility.

Agility

But what do we actually mean by agility? *Agile* literally translates as "the ability to move quickly and easily." In the context of this book, it is expressed by terms such as dexterity, flexibility, lightness, speed, sharpness, strength, focus, precision, and adaptability. The aim of agility is adaptivity, the responsive capacity of the organization to adapt to new requirements: to be ready for anything.

Compare it with a chameleon. These insect-eating reptiles are a very successful survivor, existing for over one hundred million years. Its success is partly due to its two independently moving eyes, with which he constantly scans the environment for food and danger. And, depending on the situation, he can, with lightning speed, adapt the color of his skin: sometimes as camouflage and sometimes to stand out, in order to scare enemies away or to find a mating partner. He has also developed an amazing tongue for catching prey: is the fastest functioning muscle in any reptile or mammal (for comparison, the 0–60 mph time of a chameleon's tongue is 1/100th of a second).[3]

If you want your organization to be as effective as a chameleon, you need to have resilience and flexibility. And, because you've got to minimize time-to-market, an undeniable *need for speed*. Not just in the island of a single team, but across the entire value chain. Any weak links will hugely slow down the whole enterprise.

The *agile management* process is meant to ensure the agility that makes the necessary adaptability achievable. It is actually a combination of agile and lean, we could call it *agilean*. As can be seen in Figure 7.1, agile management forms the integrated, facilitative basis for:

- *Maintenance*–These are the activities of the organization aimed at maintaining current technological, managerial, and operational standards, for example via training and discipline. Maintenance is the responsibility of everyone in the organization. The rule of thumb is that the organization must spend about half its time on this.
- *Continuous improvement*–The activities intended to enhance technological, managerial, and operational standards, over the longer term, through small, daily steps. This, too, is a responsibility of everyone in the organization. About one-third of the organization's time should be spent here.

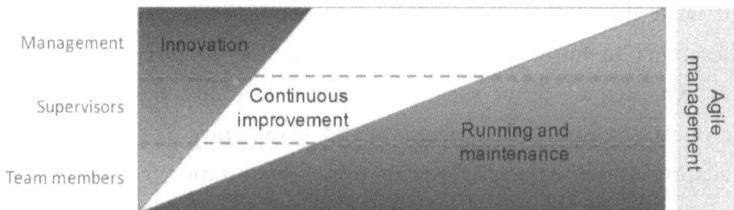

Figure 7.1 Agile management facilitates all business processes (based on Imai[4])

- *Innovation*–Defined here as dramatic improvements in the short term, due to relatively large and targeted investment, and is the responsibility of middle and top management. This occupies about one-sixth of the organization's time.

In this way, agile management is the basis for both operational activities and projects, as you will see later in the Spotify and ING case studies. It is aimed at both internal and external customers.

7.2   For Internal and External Customers

It is very important to understand that agile management applies not only to external customers, but also to internal customers. Obviously, the external customer is central in agile management: the one who pays everyone's salaries. Everything within the organization, therefore, should be aimed at creating maximum added value for the external customer. And that is exactly why the internal customer is relevant, as you can see in Figure 7.2.

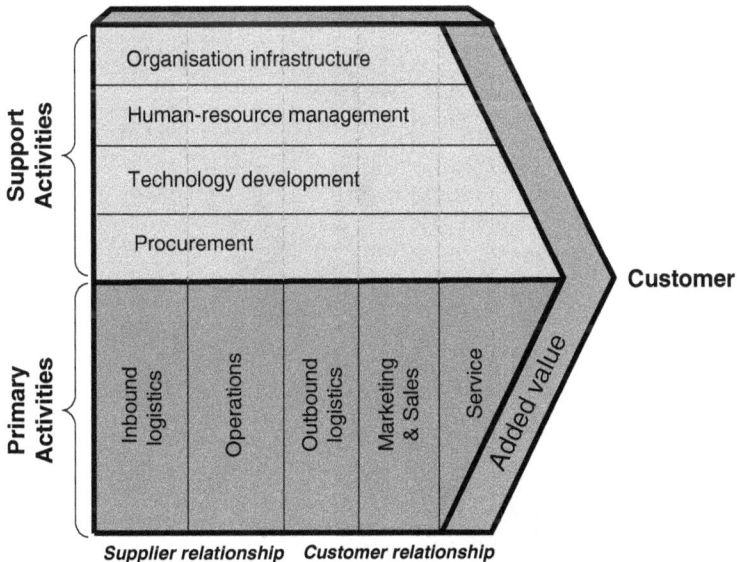

Figure 7.2 Porter's value-chain model shows how customer value is created

The interplay of internal processes ensures the organization, as a whole, can create added value for the external customer. The better these internal processes are aligned, the more-effectively and efficiently the organization creates added value for the external customer. This means that departments that are not directly customer-facing do indeed serve a customer: the internal. Each internal customer is the next step in the value-creation cycle. The output of a process conducted by one department becomes the input for the next process, either in the same or a different department. And thus, one process is always the customer of the preceding process. The better these internal customers are served, the more value is created for the end (external) customer. It is, therefore, important that work activities focus on both internal and external customers. Excellent tools for ensuring this takes place are *value-stream mapping* and the *business-model canvas*, as we shall see in Chapter 10.

But what is the relevance of agile management for departments with internal customers? It is found in the logic of the "domino effect" (see Figure 7.3). If changes occur in the behavior of the customer or the market, the customer-facing departments of the organization will notice it first. Sales and customer service would be forced to adapt their methods the most quickly, with consequences for the departments of which they are internal customers. These

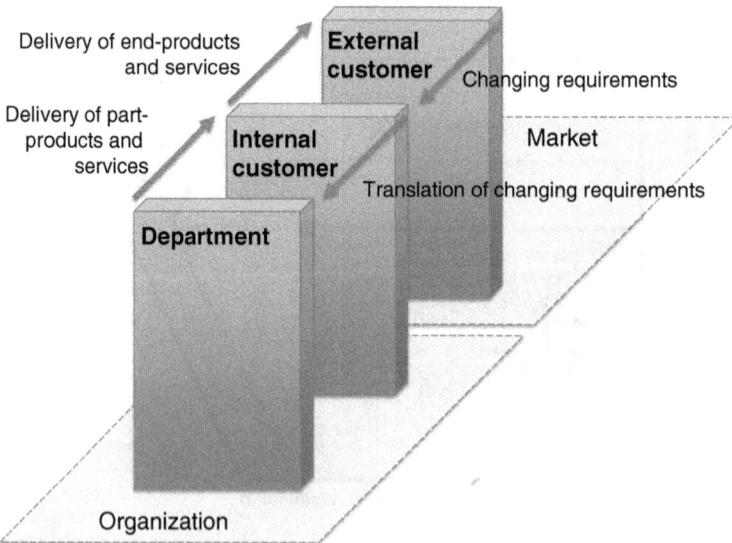

Figure 7.3 The domino-effect of changing requirements

internal departments must quickly adapt their processes to meet the new requirements of sales and customer service, and so on.

Agile management is not an all-or-nothing choice. Although full implementation is of course the ideal situation, it is perfectly possible to choose a customized hybrid model where some departments use it while others continue to work in the traditional way. The latter are usually very small or responsible for mostly simple, repetitive tasks with fixed outcomes (which can be optimized through "lean" methods). Nor is the form of implementation cast in concrete. Above a certain minimum level, it is a flexible model. This means during experimentation, each organization will discover what best suits it. In other words, you can apply an agile management approach to implementing agile management.

In short, every employee, to a greater or lesser extent, will be involved in agile management. The next section discusses the principles that should be followed.

7.3   The Eight Principles of Agile Management

Agile management is an iterative, incremental way of working that creates a responsive organization. *Iterative* means that work is done in systematic, repeatable, process steps, accepting that sometimes a step needs to be done again, because insight has identified that it began with a false premise. *Incremental* means that only a little is added to what already exists, whether that is a product or an insight. As we saw in section 6.1, the principle of building on what is available can be found in the foundations of science. Isaac Newton once said: "If I have seen further, it is by standing on the shoulders of giants."

The goal is not explicitly to achieve a large, radical leap forward in one go. Of course this sometimes happens, because you accidentally discover something fundamentally new. However, the starting point is that, together, many quick, small steps add up to a big leap forward, but with much less initial risk and uncertainty. This idea is based on eight key principles, which we discuss below.

1. *Creating value*

   The highest priority is value for customers through rapid and continuous delivery of new or renewed products and services. These are working solutions that offer relevant experience. This applies for both internal and external customers.

- Creating value for the customer means working "lean"; therefore any activity the customer is not willing to pay for must be eliminated. To avoid unnecessary investments and long lead times, work aims to produce so-called *minimum viable products;* these allow the customer to experience the essence of the benefits of a product or service.

2. *Understanding the customer*

In order to create value for internal or external customers, it is necessary to understand their requirements, needs, and behaviors.

- The customers completely self-determine the relevance and value of the experiences and solutions offered. It is impossible to do so on the basis of internal assumptions. Therefore, it is necessary to understand the wishes, needs, and the behaviors of the target group. These can be examined with the aid of *voice-of-the-customer* tools as feedback sources.

3. *Alignment*

Creating value for the customer requires that the customer is given a central position in the close collaboration of a team that comprises stakeholders from all relevant departments. This team should be motivated and should share a common vision of success.

- Much of the value-creation is lost if the client experience is chopped up into separate soloed departments. Therefore, a multidisciplinary internal collaboration, around customers and their behavior, is necessary and this should be sponsored at the highest organizational level. The team members must be convinced of the usefulness of the overarching objectives that transcend the interests of their own departments. And if several multidisciplinary teams are involved, agreement must also be made, between those teams, to coordinate their goals and activities.

4. *Empowerment*

The team should get all the support and autonomy it needs, removing any external obstacles and giving it the full trust and mandate to do the job independently. This gives the team *end-to-end* responsibility for achieving its goals. Daring to trust each other increases the speed of collaboration.

- Management's main role is to facilitate teams. This includes resolving issues that go beyond the team level, so the team can focus entirely on its tasks. Checking on assignments only "before and after," empowers the team and its leaders, allowing them full freedom to carry out their work in a self-organizing way. Micro-management is thus counterproductive.

5. *Synchronous and visual communication*

   The most efficient and effective way to share information with or within the team is via synchronous communication-preferably face-to-face.[5] And to make everything as visual as possible.

   - Teams operate best when team members can communicate quickly and directly with each other. This means that the ideal working environment consists of a shared space where all team members are physically together. The space should also have a visual overview of all relevant activities, including a prioritized schedule that team members briefly update to each other at the start of each day.

6. *Learning by experimenting*

   The most important measure of progress is learning via a structured cycle, and this requires accurate measurement. Experimentation and failure form an important part of learning, and should therefore be unanimously accepted.

   - The focus is on continuous improvement, requiring a structured process in which experimenting is central. To generate maximum learning, working with hypotheses, SMART goals, precise measurements, analyses, and evaluations is strictly necessary. In addition, all stakeholders must feel safe to dare to make mistakes, because these are a calculated risk.

7. *Speed and flexibility*

   Change should be considered as a source of opportunity. This is taken into account in the planning and in the focus on simplicity and quality, because the ability to respond quickly to changes is a source of competitive advantage.

   - To test ideas as quickly and cheaply as possible, and with the help of the 80/20 rule, work is managed using "sketches" instead of thick, rigid plans. And by deploying short-cycles with small, incremental additions to products, services, and experiences. These additions should, as simply as possible, show the essence, omitting anything unnecessary. Additions and changes are picked up, at a constant pace, from the ideas pipeline and delivered within a few weeks, which makes for flexibility. The work is then checked continuously against the agreed minimum quality levels.

8. *Accountability*

The team activities should be *accountable*. After each iteration, the team honestly evaluates all its activities and results, adjusting its plans and activities accordingly.

- The team also has a meta-goal, to learn as much as possible about its own functioning. Therefore, team members ensure transparency in their work and they periodically review the added value it is generating. Where necessary, the team optimizes its approach so that return-on-effort continuously improves.

Figure 7.4 shows that these eight principles form the core values of agile management.

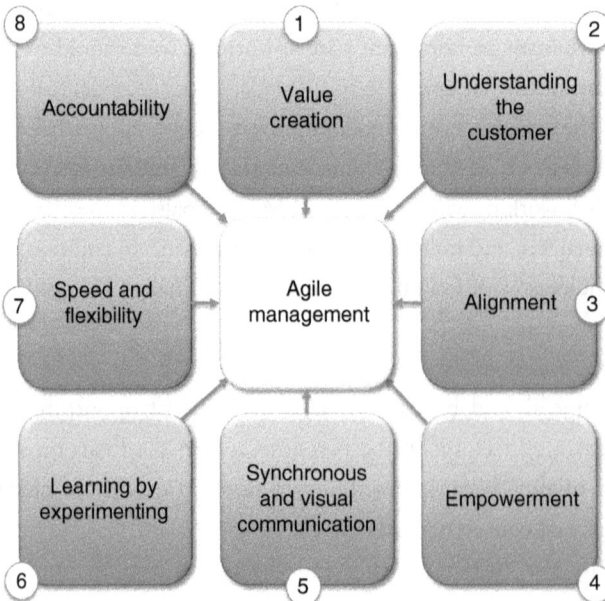

Figure 7.4 The eight principles of agile management

As you will see later in this book, an extensive toolbox is available of methods and concepts to apply agile management principles in the daily practice of your organization. But, naturally, it all begins with culture and leadership. You can read more about this in the next section.

7.4   Culture and Leadership: Working Together Differently

Often you hear managers complain: Why don't my employees take the initiative more often? Why do they seem not really concerned? Why don't they show entrepreneurship? Why is their motivation so low? And so on.

What these executives are often unaware of is that, unconsciously, they are maintaining the situation themselves.[6] It is a self-fulfilling prophecy. As we saw in chapter 3, managers increasingly focus on the short term, on efficiency and predictability. They seek stability in order to achieve the results promised to stakeholders. Surprises are thereby not appreciated. That's why they want to hold onto the security that traditional hierarchical structures and processes provide, which are mostly product-oriented instead of customer-oriented. They fall into the trap of directly controlling their employees, determining, top-down, what their people must do and how they must do it. They do not dare to trust their employees (see the YouTube video *The smell of the place* for a brilliant illustration).

The consequence is that employees dutifully perform what is asked of them. They become passive and do not feel "ownership." Leaders see that progress does not go fast enough or well enough to get the necessary results, so they start to get themselves involved. They take the employees chair and begin working with content and details. They're micro-managing.

This has the consequence that employees become uncertain, afraid to make mistakes, and do not dare to take responsibility. Their motivation disappears, resulting in, for example, slowness, errors, and defensive behaviors. Often a political atmosphere develops: there is tension with and between the managers, who reflexively lapse deeper into old patterns. They become even more hands-on, take the initiative away from their employees while plaguing them with inspections and monitoring. And the result? Even more bureaucracy.

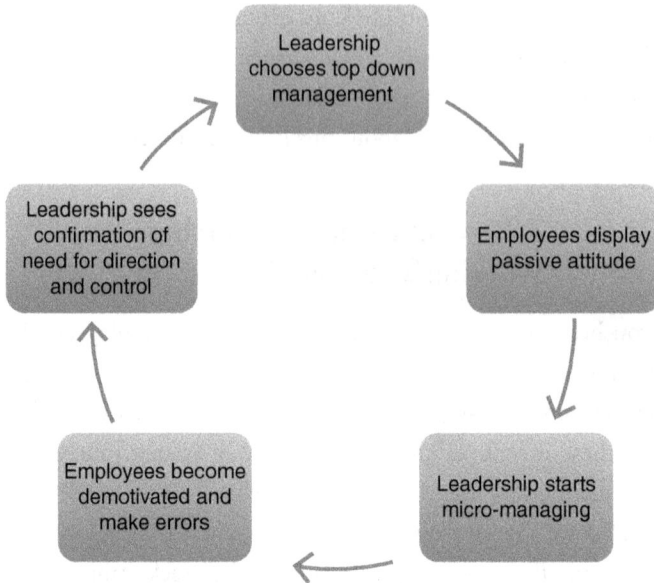

Figure 7.5 The vicious circle of directive control

The selective perception of executives confirms their original starting point: the need to focus on the short term, on efficiency and predictability. Now, as Figure 7.5 shows, they are all in a vicious circle.

From Directive to Servant Leadership

What we see, in the above situation, is a negative spiral. But how do we break through it? And might it even be possible to create a virtuous circle? Organizations that work with agile management have, indeed, shown that you can. These organizations opt for a bottom-up approach. Within the framework of their mission, vision, and strategy, they try to incentivize employee entrepreneurship as far as possible. A culture of "do first, and ask (permission or offer apologies) afterwards"; the *art of letting go*. They achieve this by creating self-organizing teams (for some inspiration see the YouTube video *Greatness* by David Marquet). That means freedom, but does not mean a lack of commitment. Delivering operating results is central. Teams and team members are given responsibility to achieve their results, but the way they do so is entirely their own choice. So there is room for initiative and entrepreneurship. This ensures high levels of motivation and productivity and improves customer service.

This means a lot for managers. First, this method usually leads to a flattening of the organizational structure: hierarchical management layers can thus be eliminated, making many executive posts redundant. Second, leadership style changes from directing to serving (as Robert Greenleaf already put it in 1904: "Good leaders must first become good servants"). The main task of management becomes to facilitate teams, as much as possible, to deliver performance. For example, by ensuring they have optimal working conditions, protecting them from less relevant and urgent issues, and so on. An important task is to motivate the team and give them confidence, encourage them to get the best out of themselves and develop themselves. Thirdly, it means that many executives become "working foremen." In addition to their management tasks, they also collaborate as a team member and carry out practical work. So, as it were, managers need to reinvent themselves.

Perhaps the greatest challenge lies in the combination of autonomy and alignment. In other words, how to realize maximum freedom for the teams and, at the same time, facilitate the necessary coordination between the teams and the strategy needed to ensure certain things do not happen— or are not duplicated. Many executives feel this as a sort of simple balance: an either/or situation. Nevertheless, it does not have to be so. Just as the leadership communicates very clearly what are the strategy, goals, and structures and how this relates to each team, they create, within the teams, a lot of freedom to go their own way. Good fences make good neighbors, as the saying goes. That is how you realize autonomy *and* alignment. And alignment is easier when there is greater visual representation of the work (you can read more about this in Section 11.2).

A good example of the issues above can be found at Patagonia and at Buurtzorg (what Frederic Laloux calls "teal" organizations[7]). But also in the Spotify story, which follows below.

7.5   Culture and Leadership within Spotify

The Swedish company Spotify was established in 2006. By now, about 100 million people in 58 countries use the music-streaming service, of which 40 million have a paid subscription. For its library of over 30 million songs, Spotify has paid a total of approximately $3 billion to the copyright holders. The most popular song to date, *One Dance*, has been streamed more than one billion times (for the top-50 songs this is 30 billion in total). Spotify is also a formidable competitor to iTunes, as we'll see in section 10.1.

Spotify now has approximately 1,900 employees in eighteen countries. In all these countries, the organization has adopted agile management. Spotify puts a particular emphasis on its culture. The organization promotes its culture by making it the focus for its agile coaches during week-long Spotify culture bootcamps for new employees and by encouraging active storytelling through presentations, blogs, and so on. The ethos of the Spotify culture is interesting to examine. Below it is discussed according to Spotify's own explanation.[8]

Principles are More Important than Rules

Spotify begins with the belief that rules are a good starting point, but not more than that. If necessary, rules may be broken or changed. This happened partly because Spotify noticed that the rules associated with its Scrum and Kanban approaches increasingly began to "pinch," to hinder rather than help as the organization grew. It now labels these rules as optional. Spotify prefers the principles of agile management over the strict procedures and rules defined within the Scrum approach (probably the remark most frequently made by Spotify employees is "It depends . . ."). Spotify has also flexibly adapted the role of Scrum Master. Instead of monitoring the quality of the process, this person focuses on facilitating and coaching the team. They call this role the *Agile Coach*.

Empowerment via Smart Alignment

Spotify works in teams of up to eight people, with end-to-end responsibility to fulfil their specific purpose. The goal could be, for example, improving the infrastructure or a particular feature. The team is fully autonomous in achieving its goal, and works within a few frameworks such as Spotify's overall mission and strategy, and with associated short-term goals that are determined each quarter. Each team has its own fixed workplace. All the offices are in one room; the side and rear walls are large whiteboards where things can be worked out visually. The front wall, on the corridor side, is made up entirely of glass in order to stimulate transparency and accessibility. Adjacent is an open lounge space for dialogue, and, behind it, a small space (the *huddle room*) a quiet space for working on something individually or with only one or two team members.

Autonomy helps to increase team spirit and motivation and avoids unnecessary meetings or discussions. At the same time, Spotify wants to prevent suboptimization. Spotify calls this principle "loosely coupled but tightly aligned." The better the alignment between the teams around their goals, the more autonomy they create for their implementation work. In addition, it helps to pursue small, frequent improvements. This ensures routine and speed and prevents the need for intensive consultation and collaboration between teams on large, complex improvement projects. Spotify calls it *decoupled releases.*

At the highest level within the organization, the leadership must therefore communicate clearly to the team what improvements should be realized (or problems solved) and why. A team must then work together to find the best solution themselves.

Trust Instead of Control

Due to the high degree of autonomy within Spotify, there is little standardization in the way they work. Each team may choose his own methods. The company relies on the effect of cross-pollination and assumes that the methods that work best will spread themselves through informal consultations between the teams, and become a de facto standard. In this way, Spotify tries to find a healthy balance between consistency and flexibility. Teams may also work on each other's products in a kind of open-source model, what one might call *self-service.* They do not have to wait for each other, quality improves and knowledge is disseminated.

Spotify wants to be more liberal than authoritative, and it accepts the risk of everything falling into chaos. If everyone dares to trust each other's good intentions, Spotify will benefit much from reduced bureaucratic control. Teams must, therefore, simply behave according to good citizenship. Spotify also wants to avoid becoming a "political" organization. Decisions, as much as possible, are based on data rather than opinions or authority.

Respect and Motivation

Spotify tries to build their organization around the human being. The company wants employees to *get* energy from working with their colleagues. This involves mutual respect, and big egos are undesirable. Employees should get recognition for their successes. Wanting to help each other well and quickly is paramount. Spotify also actively tries to keep employee motivation as high as possible, so has discontinued project-time estimates and time registration. For example, Spotify uses "guilds"; these are platforms for special interests in which employees can voluntarily take part in the form of events and forums. Spotify wants to build "communities" where employees feel a sense of belonging, because it does not really believe in the value of organizational structures. Also, every employee gets 10 percent *hack time* to work on its own ideas and projects.

Experimenting, Failing, and Learning

Spotify's basic belief is that it wants to fail as soon as possible, and thereby learn and improve quickly. Teams and employees should have no fear of failure. Spotify doesn't want to prevent failures, but does want to be able to recover from them quickly. Mistakes and failures are displayed on *fail walls* and extensively discussed in the team's *retrospective* discussions. Not to establish whose fault it was, but to see what everyone can learn from it and what needs to be changed. Continuous improvement is central.

The *decoupled releases,* we encountered earlier, ensure failures always have a limited impact on the customer and they are quickly recovered. Spotify calls this the *limited blast radius.* Also releases are rolled-out in steps to small groups of customers and are closely monitored in order to intervene quickly if something goes wrong.

To encourage further learning, Spotify also uses the Lean Startup approach in its own experimental cycle *think it-build it-ship it-tweak it.*

Here, one works with *hypotheses, minimum viable products,* and A/B testing analysis. Innovation and impact are more important than predictability and reliable planning. Constantly trying out new things is not only for products, but also for their own methods and processes. Many teams use a "kata-board" (borrowed from Lean) in which they describe the current problems and desired future state. They also describe the next step toward that situation and the three key activities that go with it.

Finally, you just heard about *hack time.* Twice a year Spotify even has a Hack Week where everyone works together on their own fun ideas. Everything is permitted and regularly, useful applications emerge from this activity. The week ends with a demo day and a big party.

By reading this chapter, you'll have discovered the following:

- *Agile management is an integrated approach to maintenance, continuous improvement, and innovation. It is aimed at both internal and external customers.*
- *Agile management is an iterative, incremental way of working that makes an organization responsive. It is based on eight principles: creating value; understanding the customer; alignment; empowerment; synchronous and visual communications; learning by experimenting; speed and flexibility; accountability.*
- *Agile management breaks the vicious circle of sending directives. Using self-organizing teams stimulates entrepreneurship. This challenges traditionally minded executives to reimagine their own roles.*
- *The Spotify case shows how such an interpretation of culture and leadership can be successful.*

You have now come to the end of Part 1 of this book. In Part 2, you can discover the methods and tools currently available to concretely implement agile management within your organization.

References

1. Hamel, G., and L. Välinkangas. (2003). *The Quest for Resilience*. Brighton: Harvard Business Review, pp. 52–63.
2. Setili, A. (2014). *The Agility Advantage*. Jossey-Bass.
3. Anderson, C. V. (2016). Off Like a Shot: Scaling or Ballistic Tongue Projection Reveals Extremely High Performance in Small Chameleons. *Nature—Scientific Reports*. http://www.nature.com/articles/srep18625, (January 6, 2016).
4. Imai, M. (2012). *Gemba Kaizen*. New York: McGraw-Hill.
5. Carpenter, C. E., and S. N. Madhavapeddi. (2008). Perceptions of Organizational Media Richness: Channel Expansion Effects for Electronic and Traditional Media across Richness Dimensions. *Professional Communication* 51, no. 1, pp. 18-32.
6. Ardon, A. (2011). *Break the circle!* Publisher Business Contact.
7. Laloux, F. (2014). *Reinventing organizations*. Millis: Nelson Parker.
8. Thanks to Henrik Kniberg; see also the two YouTube videos about the "Spotify engineering culture." (Also on the corporate culture of Zappos.com example can be found on YouTube inspiring videos.)

PART 2

Agile Management—Putting It into Practice

Let's get started!

Now you know exactly what agile management is and offers, you probably want to use it in your organization. But how do you do that? In Part 2, you'll learn all about it by looking at questions such as:

- How do I organize my organization?
- How do I make the transformation from our current situation?
- Which processes do I need to apply and how do I apply them?
- What specific tools are available for identifying our areas for improvement and how do I prioritize these improvements?
- How do I determine if the improvements I make deliver the desired result?
- What is the easiest way to build the improvements and then implement them?
- How do I avoid wasting time and money in improvements that do not seem to work? And how can I actually test whether they work well?
- What information resources can I use for the above?
- How should I deploy the information gathered from these resources, to best evaluate our efforts and results?
- What should I do if the results are disappointing? And what if they are good, or perhaps even better than hoped for?

CHAPTER 8

The Agile Organization

The best way to predict your future is to create it.
                                                    —Abraham Lincoln

Welcome to the second part of this book, which focuses on the real-world application of agile management. This first chapter looks at how to translate the agile principles from Chapter 7 into your new organizational structure.

8.1   Organizing for Agile Management

It is 1980 when the Brazilian, Antonio Semler, asks his son Ricardo to start working in his company, Semco, which produces industrial mixers and turns over $4 million annually. Ricardo is 21 years old and really only interested in playing guitar with his rock band; but he agrees. Within a week, however, father and son are already having a blazing row. Ricardo sees passive, unhappy workers, who are doing boring work, are strictly controlled and are totally uninspired, just waiting until it is time to clock out. According to Ricardo, this is a result of the autocratic way in which his father runs the company and he, therefore, wants to make this more democratic. After yet another of their regular arguments, his father decides to retire and give Ricardo the freedom he wants. And he takes it too. He immediately dismisses most of the managers, abolishes the hierarchical structure, and diversifies the company into other sectors. He starts building a culture where reliability, honesty, transparency, and trust are key. His main goal is to have happy employees, because he believes that everything else will follow naturally. Therefore, workers are free to do whatever they want, within the framework of the company's mission, as long as the job is completed on time. They share in the profits, set their own salaries, and determine their own working hours. They are encouraged to dare, to be creative, and to investigate and question everything. And to recognize their own mistakes, guided by the principle that everything can be improved, always. Sales grow dramatically by 25 percent to 40 percent per year. Semco now boasts eight separate companies, with around five thousand employees, and all are market leaders in their industry. According to Ricardo Semler, these results are directly attributable to what he calls self-organization.[1]

Self-Organization

In many European countries, traffic signs and lights are increasingly being removed, especially at intersections. The idea behind this is *shared space*. The premise is respect rather than rules: road users are perfectly able to work with each other to ensure everything runs smoothly. And it seems to work: there is more communication and safety improves. You can also see it in shops and restaurants. Long ago, it was thought that shop-assistants were the only possible way to let customers buy something. When the first self-service stores opened, almost nobody believed this concept could work. But customers proved well able to control most things they needed to, and it came with more speed and cost savings. Nowadays, it is so obvious that it works, that many people prefer not to be helped by an assistant. We do it all ourselves, in supermarkets, gas stations, McDonald's, and Ikea, but also online and even, step-by-digital-step creating our ideal vacation. You can compare it to making music: a big classical orchestra must have a conductor, but a small jazz orchestra or a rock band can "jam" together perfectly without one.

Self-organization can be a success factor for organizations if their structures are established around small, independent groups. This is based on "Dunbar's number," the insight that the number of people with whom one can maintain relationships is cognitively limited.[2]

The potential of self-organization is proved by the "lattice" (or "open allocation") management concept that W. L. Gore & Associates deploys, which is comparable to the "cell philosophy" applied within BSO, and Zappos' "holacracy" approach.

If you dare to let go of control, you create a lot of space. And with the right care and stimulation, good things will arise to fill that space. Things that remained contained when there was no space for them to appear and flourish. Very likely, your employees then experience more job satisfaction, feel more involved, have more initiative, are more productive, more innovative, and deliver better quality. Agile management is not an end in itself, but a means to achieve these benefits. You want your people to work with head, heart, and hands. And self-organization is a foundation for this. Figure 8.1 shows us, based on extensive scientific literature,[3] where we should put our attention when we want to make our organizations agile.

The *People* success factor includes the elements of culture and leadership we discussed in Chapter 7. *Processes* are covered in Chapter 9 onwards; below you can read more about *organizational structures* and *information systems*.

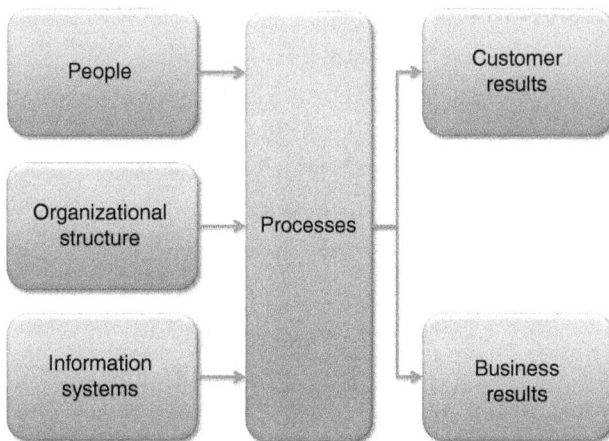

Figure 8.1 The four success factors of agile management and their impact on the results

Organizational structures

To stimulate entrepreneurship within agile management, you work with self-organizing, cross-functional teams. These can range in size from three to ten people, but seven or eight is ideal. The teams consist of employees, from different disciplines, who together are responsible for achieving a specific goal from start to end. Goals can be large or small, wide-ranging or very specific: developing a new market or product, optimum implementation of human resource management (HRM) policy, getting the most out of an enterprise resource planning (ERP) system, or providing the best possible instore customer experience. A priority is that the team must always learn from what they do, and that proceeds most effectively in groups.[4] Eventually, this learning leads to value for the customer; internal or external.

Therefore, you need a team of different specialists. Compare it with professional football: the goalkeeper, defenders, midfielders, and forwards need to cooperate closely and each must make their specific contribution. But even if you have the best players, you still need other specialist roles. There are the coaches, skills trainers, condition and strength trainers, equipment managers, physiotherapists, doctors, psychologists, and many more. All are aiming to get the team performing optimally. And it works the same in agile management. Often people choose to work with organizational roles that originated in Scrum, sometimes with custom names and responsibilities (see ING's case study in section 8.3).

Beside the team members, the roles globally look as follows:

- *Product owner*—This is the principal of the team. He determines which products/services are to be developed and, within this, what are the priorities for the *product backlog* (you'll read more about this below). Also he must have the necessary budget for the purpose. When he brings all the above, he creates clarity and calm.
- *Agile coach*—The agile coach ensures that the team gets continually better at applying agile-management principles. He also ensures that the environment of the team, inside and outside the organization, not only does not hinder team success, but contributes positively to it. He is emphatically not a project manager, because

the team members jointly fill that function. The agile coach is a "servant" to the team, focused on facilitating it, and at the same time can be a team member contributing to the team goal.

If the organization is large, with multiple agile teams, you often see the role emerge of "agile manager" (see the *Tribe Lead* in the ING case study). An important goal for the agile manager is to steer the teams into alignment between each other without limiting their autonomy, as we saw with Spotify. Too much freedom leads to chaos and suboptimization, for example, because activities overlap or counteract each other. Therefore, the agile manager must create the kind of framework that he trusts will allow the team to work with the most freedom possible. He creates clarity by communicating regularly about the organization's goals, and the associated subgoals of each team. He must also monitor the *flow* speed, as it affects how much value teams can create in their mutual value chains. He needs to keep the *product owners* informed and in agreement by regularly arranging so-called *sync/huddle meetings*, of which you can read more later. For larger, more complex situations, specific monitoring tools have been developed, such as SAFe (*Scaled Agile Framework*) and LeSS (*Large Scale Scrum*),[5] but these, however, up until now, have been specifically focused on software development.

Finally, alongside organizing agile management, you also need to arrange for *governance*. Specifically, this means translating the organization's strategy and vision into clear goals (OKRs) for the teams. The teams need to render these goals into specific key performance indicators (KPIs) for their efforts and results, indicators which put customer value-creation, learning, and quality central. After each iteration, the team should report back in a practical way, using reporting-structures that can simply become the basis for communication with internal and external stakeholders. Furthermore, all the processes and consultations are subject to continual refinement, as you will see in Chapter 9 and onwards. The same applies to HRM tools, such as personal development plans, evaluation processes, and reward mechanisms.

In the case of *governance*, it is of interest for the management to look at the performance of the value chain as a whole, rather than at the individual components. Agility does not ignore the fact that a chain is only as strong as its weakest link.

The Crucial Role of Information Technology

IT plays an enormously important role within agile management. Firstly, in-house or external IT professionals must work together with business functions in order to deliver the technology involved in customer solutions. These people should also be included in the multidisciplinary teams. Often within the IT organization, there is existing experience with agile working (usually Scrum). This makes cooperation easier and, therefore, offers opportunities to learn from existing agile knowledge and experience.

Secondly, information systems are necessary to quickly and accurately capture, measure, and analyze customer behavior, for instance via *digital analytics*. It is desirable to do this at all *touchpoints* and to integrate it completely into a 360 degree view of customer behavior. This is best achieved by smart-linking systems such as CRM, data warehousing, and analytics.

8.2   Agile Assessment: How Agile Is Your Organization Right Now?

Chances are you are curious about how agile your own organization currently is. You can find this out immediately below, by reading each proposition and determining the extent to which it applies to your organization. Via this science-based methodology, you build a picture of your organization, based on identifying your strengths and weaknesses.

You now have two choices:

- *Do the self-assessment now*
  The advantage here is that you can do this reasonably objectively, without being influenced by the content in Part 2, so you'll probably give the most accurate and least socially desirable answers. The downside of course is that you might be still unclear about some concepts and this might affect your ability to answer from a full understanding.

- *Do the self-assessment when you have finished reading Part 2 of this book.*

  The opposite applies here: because you know exactly what the content is about, this can influence how you answer the questions.

It's your choice (as the great Dutch footballer, Johan Cruyff, would say: "Every disadvantage has its advantage"). Whichever approach you choose for your self-assessment, you can use Table 8.1. For every statement with which you agree or disagree, indicate the level by placing a cross (X) in the appropriate box. You can fill in the questions from a broad or narrow perspective, as you wish: for a team, for a department, a business unit, or your entire organization. You can find an online version of this self-assessment at agilemanaging.org under *Research*.

Now you have filled-in your answers, it is time to analyze the results. This can be done using Table 8.2. The upper half concerns questions 1 to 33. First, count the number of crosses you made by category ("Completely disagree"—"Completely agree") in Table 8.1 and write these numbers in the appropriate boxes. Multiply this category number by the corresponding value for that category (1–5) to calculate the cumulative value, and record your cumulative values in the appropriate boxes. Calculate the total by adding these five numbers together and write this number in the appropriate box. Finally, divide this number by 33 and then multiply it by 20.

Table 8.1 Self-assessing the agility of your organization

1. Completely disagree; 2. Disagree; 3. Neutral; 4. Agree; 5. Completely agree; 6. Not applicable		Assessment					
	Indicator	1	2	3	4	5	6
1	Our teams have to use customer input for identifying improvement opportunities for our products, services, and channels.						
2	Our teams should use input from customers to prioritize the improvement opportunities for our products, services, and channels.						
3	Our teams have to develop improvements to products, services, and channels in short cycles (up to four weeks).						

(Continued)

Table 8.1 Self-assessing the agility of your organization (Continued)

	Indicator	Assessment					
		1	2	3	4	5	6
4	Within our processes, a mechanism is available which allows customers to give feedback on the improvements to products, services, and channels we have developed.						
5	Our teams must ensure the improvements to products, services, and channels that have been developed during a cycle are accepted by their client.						
6	We provide our teams with tools to test the developed improvements of our products, services, and channels with our customers.						
7	Our teams are made up of stakeholders from all parts of the organization, who are relevant to the improvement of products, services, and channels.						
8	We have defined an approach for optimal assembling of teams based on the expertise needed.						
9	If a person, from a part of the organization, which is relevant to the improvement of products, services, and channels, cannot be part of the development team, he or she must always be readily available to consult.						
10	Prior to a development cycle, our teams should allocate time to jointly prioritize the developing of improvements to products, services, and channels.						
11	Prior to a development cycle, our teams should allocate time to the joint planning of activities within a development cycle.						
12	Our teams have to allocate time every day to jointly discuss the progress of activities within a development cycle.						
13	At the end of a development cycle, our teams should allocate time to jointly evaluate the activities and results of the completed development cycle.						
14	We provide our teams with tools for capturing the results of the evaluation taking place at the end of a development cycle.						

Table 8.1 Self-assessing the agility of your organization (Continued)

	Indicator	1	2	3	4	5	6
		Assessment					
15	Our employees need to communicate and collaborate face-to-face with their colleagues within and between teams.						
16	Our teams work in a physical environment that facilitates them to communicate and collaborate face-to-face.						
17	Our teams should define, plan, and control their daily activities themselves.						
18	Within a team, employees must demonstrate individual or collective ownership for the improvements they have developed in products, services, or channels.						
19	Our teams have established agreements with their management regarding their performance.						
20	Our management supports the self-organizing nature of the teams.						
21	Our teams must use a clearly defined approach to determine the desired improvements to our products, services, and channels.						
22	Our teams need to use a clearly defined approach to estimate the amount of work that will be performed during a development cycle.						
23	Our teams must use a clearly defined approach to translate the improvements to our products, services, and channels into *user stories* (simple descriptions of the *requirements* from a customer perspective).						
24	Our teams must use a clearly defined approach to prioritizing improvements, *user stories*, and tasks in a development cycle.						
25	Our teams have to create a schedule for each development cycle.						
26	Our teams must estimate the time required for any improvement to our products, services, and channels and associated *user stories*.						
27	Our teams have, at their disposal, tools for capturing the content of improvements to our products, services, and channels and associated *user stories*.						

(Continued)

Table 8.1 Self-assessing the agility of your organization (Continued)

	Indicator	Assessment 1	2	3	4	5	6
28	At the start, our teams must determine only the global characteristics of improvements to our products, services, and channels.						
29	Our teams must follow an evolutionary approach in designing improvements to our products, services, and channels instead of fully designing these in advance.						
30	Our teams must determine and refine requirements for enhancements to our products, services, and channels at the last possible moment (*just-in-time*).						
31	We provide our teams with tools to maintain documentation on their activities and their results.						
32	Our teams need to keep minimal documentation about their activities and their results.						
33	Our teams are receptive to keeping minimal documentation about their activities and their results.						
34	Our customers provide input for prioritizing improvement opportunities for our products, services, and channels.						
35	Until now, improvements made to our products, services, and channels meet the expectations of our customers.						
36	The wishes expressed, up until now, by our customers for improvements to our products, services, and channels have already been realized or will be realized shortly.						
37	We deliver improvements to our products, services, and channels to our customers in short cycles of up to four weeks.						
38	Completed improvements to our products, services, and channels have not been reversed.						
39	Our customers give feedback on the improvements we have developed to products, services, and channels.						
40	Our teams test the improvements, developed by them to our products, services, and channels, with our customers.						

Table 8.1 *Self-assessing the agility of your organization (Continued)*

	Indicator	Assessment					
		1	2	3	4	5	6
41	The time allocated prior to a development cycle to jointly prioritize the improvements to be developed to our products, services, and channels is spent by our teams in an effective way.						
42	The time allocated prior to a development cycle to the joint planning of activities within a development cycle is spent by our teams in an effective way.						
43	The time allocated daily to jointly discuss the progress of the activities within a development cycle is spent by our teams in an effective way.						
44	The time allocated at the end of a development cycle to jointly evaluate the activities and results of the completed development cycle is spent by our teams in an effective way.						
45	The above meetings of our teams for prioritizing, planning, and evaluation take place according to schedule.						
46	The above meetings of our teams for prioritizing, planning, and evaluation begin and end on time.						
47	Within our organization, communication between employees within a team is mainly face-to-face.						
48	Within our organization, communication between a team and its client is mainly face-to-face.						
49	Within our organization, communication between teams is mainly face-to-face.						
50	Within our organization, there is direct communication between the teams and our customers.						
51	During their evaluation meetings at the end of their development cycles, our teams have identified approaches that have worked well and should, therefore, be used in the future.						
52	During their evaluation meetings at the end of their development cycles, our teams have identified approaches that have not completely met expectations and have, therefore, been discontinued.						

(Continued)

Table 8.1 *Self-assessing the agility of your organization (Continued)*

	Indicator	1	2	3	4	5	6
		| Assessment					
53	During their evaluation meetings at the end of their development cycles, our teams have identified approaches that might better meet the needs of the teams.						
54	Our teams have fully achieved the goals they set during their evaluation meetings, at the end of their development cycles.						
55	Our team members have the necessary expertise to complete their assigned tasks.						
56	The tasks assigned to our team members match their expertise.						
57	Our teams complete the work to which they have committed in an effective manner.						
58	Our team members are able to help each other in performing their tasks.						
59	Our teams are not dependent on knowledge from outside the team.						
60	Our teams themselves determine the amount of work they perform.						
61	Our team members demonstrate ownership for the tasks assigned to them.						
62	Our team members hold each other accountable for the tasks they must complete.						
63	Our team members ensure that they complete the tasks for which they are held accountable.						
64	Our teams define, plan, and control their own daily activities without or under minimal supervision by management.						
65	Our team members form ad hoc groups at the last possible moment (*just-in-time*) to define and refine the requirements to develop improvements to our products, services, and channels.						
66	Our teams appear to make accurate estimates regarding the amount of work they can complete during a development cycle.						
67	Our development cycles are *time-boxed*.						
68	Our development cycles last four weeks or less.						
69	Our teams maintain a "development cycle backlog" (visual status list) of the activities to be carried out during the development cycle.						

Table 8.1 Self-assessing the agility of your organization (Continued)

	Indicator	Assessment 1	2	3	4	5	6
70	Our teams prioritize *user stories* when they add them to the "development cycle backlog."						
71	Our teams have fully estimated the work needed for the *user stories* before they add them to the "development cycle backlog."						
72	Our teams maintain a product backlog (an overview of improvements to products, services, and channels to be developed in future development cycles).						
73	Our teams prioritize future improvements to our products, services, and channels as they add them to the "product backlog."						
74	Our teams ensure future improvements to our products, services, and channels that have the highest priority, are always translated into *user stories* before they add them to the "product backlog."						
75	Our teams reprioritize improvement opportunities for our products, services, and channels as new opportunities for improvement are identified.						
76	Our teams only determine in advance global characteristics of improvements to our products, services, and channels.						
77	When developing improvements to our products, services, and channels, our teams work with requirements that might evolve on the basis of progressive insights.						
78	Our teams maintain minimal documentation about their activities and their results.						

This gives you your percentage, which you put in the appropriate box. This is your score. Repeat the above steps for questions 34 to 78 and write the score in the bottom half of Table 8.2.

The first score indicates how well your organization is able to create the conditions that facilitate an agile organization. If you want to improve that, you can start looking at Table 8.1, at those of the 1–33 questions to which you gave a low score (i.e., "Totally disagree," "Disagree," or "Neutral").

Table 8.2 Analysis of the results of your self-assessment

	Answers	Completely disagree	Disagree	Neutral	Agree	Completely agree
	Value	1	2	3	4	5
Facilitation—questions 1–33	Number of answers ticked to questions 1–33					
	Cumulative value (number of answers ticked times value)					
	Total (sum of all cumulative values)					
	Score (total divided by 33 and then multiplied by 20)	percent				
Effectiveness—questions 34–78	Number of answers ticked to questions 34–78					
	Cumulative value (number of answers ticked times value)					
	Total (sum of all cumulative values)					
	Score (total divided by 45 and then multiplied by 20)	percent				

The second score indicates the effectiveness of the agility of your organization. In other words: what is the result? This score can be increased by either optimizing collaboration of teams within a chain, or by improving facilitation. For the latter, go back again to Table 8.1 and look for any of 1–33 to which you gave a low score. Success!

8.3   Organizational Structure and Roles within ING Netherlands

Agile management is not restricted to start-ups and small organizations, in case you might think so. There are plenty of large organizations using this method successfully. Notable examples include Spotify, Google, Netflix, and Zappos.com: all pure online players. However, there are also large traditional organizations that work agile. The book's earlier examples of McDonald's and GE are not the only ones. Organizations like Boeing, Philips, and ING all use forms of agile management. Let's take a closer look at the last one, ING.[6] (Advance warning: in this company, the agile management approach is already quite mature. It has already been scaled-up to a large part of the organization and the *governance* for this purpose has also been continually refined. Most other organizations, however, are still in the early stages and probably see this example as a "future state."

Background and Goals

ING headquarters sees a quickly changing world, driven especially by technological developments. Customer behavior is changing because customers have more channels at their disposal to do their business, and they take it for granted that these are available 24/7 from wherever they happen to be. This results in ING feeling the need to respond quickly to changing customer needs by substantially shortening time-to-market of improvements in customer processes, so the bank can offer a more relevant and best-in-class personal service. ING hopes this approach will increasingly differentiate it from its competitors.

Solution

To achieve this, ING wants less thinking about and working on large and long-term projects and much more focus on small and short-term projects. In addition, they want fewer obstacles, transfers, and meetings between departments. Organizational silos need to be broken down in order to promote cooperation. ING wants to transfer from a *talking and thinking* culture to a *doing* culture. Instead of spending time on meetings and monitoring, ING wants to empower employees. This means more initiative and responsibility for teams and individuals, allowing ING to adapt flexibly to the needs and demands of the moment. The customer must be central.

Actualization and Implementation

ING wants the customer to experience tangible improvements. In order to achieve rapid results, they choose to follow a process cycle similar to that of many start-ups, the three steps of *think–try–adjust*. Failures are also permitted, because they can be quickly adjusted and improved. ING wants employees to be energized by discovering things together.

ING decides to fundamentally reorganize its headquarters, with *agile working* as the starting point. The bank wants people to work in small teams, which have plain, clear goals and end-to-end responsibility. These small teams should take center stage, while the organization around these teams should aim to optimally support the team in achieving its goals. In addition, it's worth noting that *agile working* is a means and not an end in itself. The premise is simple: if it does not work, make flexible adjustments, or look for another solution.

Organizational Structure

As seen in Figure 8.2, ING shapes and focuses its organization using building blocks called *squads, chapters,* and *tribes* (and no, staff members aren't swaggering around in metal-studded leather jackets with pictures of a lion and the letters ING embroidered across their backs). The characteristics of these groups are as follows.

THE AGILE ORGANIZATION   113

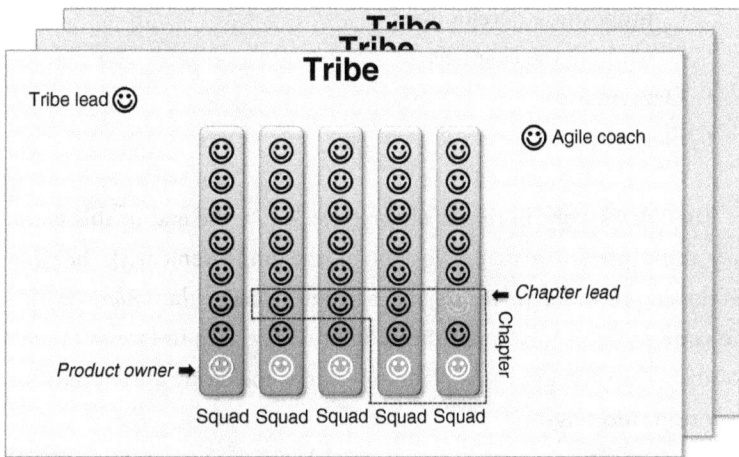

Figure 8.2 The structure of ING's agile organization is composed of squads, chapters, and tribes

Squads are self-organizing, autonomous teams with end-to-end responsibility to achieve very specific customer-related goals. An example of a "squad" is *Mortgage Applications Process*. This squad's goal is to constantly create the most customer-friendly and efficient process to get a mortgage application approved. The *Search* squad must create the most customer-friendly and effective search functionality for ING's digital channels.

Do you remember the old TV series *The A-Team*? Those men always knew how, with limited resources, to find very quick solutions to major problems. That was largely because they were complementary in their specialties (and, of course, because the *bad guys* couldn't shoot straight). A squad works on the same principle. Each is a multidisciplinary team consisting of up to nine people. The skills and expertise of the squad are determined by its goals:

- Marketing:
  - product management
  - process management
- Customer journey experts in the fields of
  - customer experience
  - customer needs

- ○ proposition development
- ○ working the channels
- Data Analysis
- IT

The *squads* work in *sprints* of three weeks. At the end of this period, they must present a demo version of the improvement(s) they have developed. In order to realize the necessary speed, the *squads* work in the same physical space, and they communicate face-to-face as much as possible. They also use visual planning boards, including during the short, daily team meetings.

Chapters run across multiple *squads*. A *chapter* is a group of up to eight members, of different *squads,* who have the same specific expertise or competence. This could be data analytics, or user experience or product management processes. *Chapters* decide for themselves how they are going to achieve their goals, and exchange knowledge and experience.

And finally, there is the *tribe:* a collection of *squads* with related goals, a kind of matrix-like structure. Examples of *tribes* are those for investments, mortgages, one-to-one propositions, private banking, daily banking, and omni-channel experience. A *tribe* may be up to 150 people. So the "Mortgages Service" *tribe* includes:

- One *squad:* Customer Journey Analysis
- Four *squads* around Mortgages Applications Process
- Five *squads* around Mortgages Management
- Four *squads* around the back-office system HYPOS
- One *squad:* Securitization (merging and subsequently selling assets and marketable securities)

Not all departments at ING's headquarters are placed into the agile organization, making it a hybrid form. For example, in the operations department, the smaller parts have been placed into a *tribe,* but its larger parts have not. And while IT staff do work within a *tribe,* hierarchically, they are part of the CIO organization. This shows its customized nature.

Roles

Within ING's *squads, chapters,* and *tribes,* everything evolves around the *squad* members. These are the employees that, as team members, contribute their specific expertise and knowledge. In addition, there are another four specific roles: *product owner, chapter lead, tribe lead,* and *agile coach.* These roles are explained in more detail below.

A *product owner* always has a business background and is responsible for one *squad.* He is not the leader of the team, but plays a functional role. He works for 90 percent of his time within the team. In his role:

- he is responsible for what the *squad* do
- he manages the *backlog* (the list of future projects) and the to-do list of ongoing projects
- he determines the priorities of the *squad.*

A *chapter lead* works for 60 percent of his time within a *squad.* He is also responsible for a *chapter.* A *chapter lead* cannot also be *product owner,* because these two roles must stay completely separate. In his role as *chapter lead*:

- he is responsible for how things are done and sets the standards for the way the team works;
- he is the hierarchical superior of the *squad* members;
- he chooses the *squad* members;
- he is responsible for the continuous personal development, coaching, and assessment cycle of the *squad* members.

A *tribe lead* has line responsibility for a *tribe* and this takes up 100 percent of his time. He coordinates the affairs of the *tribe*:

- he sets clear goals and priorities;
- he creates optimal conditions, so that *squads* can achieve their goals;
- he allocates available resources, including budget;

- he ensures coordination and cooperation between different *squads;*
- he facilitates sharing of knowledge and insights;
- he ensures coordination with other *tribes;*
- he holds weekly meetings with the *product owners* about progress in achieving their *squad's* goals;
- he gives guidance to the *chapter leads*, with whom he jointly determines the deployment of employees within the *tribe.*

Finally, there is a "loose" role, that of *agile coach.* He:

- trains and educates individuals in agile working; and
- coaches individuals and *squads* (between three and five), to improve and realize the desired *high-performance.*

Now that you know more about how you can set-up your organization, it is time to look at which process your organization should begin working on. This comes in the following chapter.

Having read this chapter, you'll have discovered the following:
- *Self-organizing teams are the foundation of agile management. The structure and management of the organization must be adapted accordingly.*
- *How agile your own organization is. You might already have determined this through a self-assessment, through which you also looked at facilitation and effectiveness.*
- *The ING Netherlands case study shows a possible structure if you want to implement agile management in your organization.*

References

1. Semler, R. (2004). *The Seven Day Weekend*. London: Portfolio
2. Also see: https://www.theguardian.com/science/2011/apr/25/few-people-dunbars-number
3. Hoogveld, M., and J. M. D. Koster. (2015). *Implementing Omnichannel Strategies: The Success Factor of Agile Processes*. Working paper.
4. Senge, P. M. (2006). *The Fifth Discipline: The Art and Practice of the Learning Organization*. New York: Doubleday.
5. See scaledagileframework.com, less.works, *disciplinedagileconsortium.org*
6. Thanks to Payam Djavdan; see also several YouTube videos about agile working at ING.

CHAPTER 9

The Agile Management Process

Think, Do, and Learn

*If everything seems under control, you're just not going
fast enough.*

—Mario Andretti

Now that you have an idea about how to structure your organization,
you are ready for the next step: establishing your methodology. You can
set these up through a simple process of three continuously repeating
steps. This section briefly discusses the purpose of these steps and explains
exactly how to implement them. In chapters 10, 11, 12, and 13, you can
find more details about these steps and associated approaches and tools.

9.1   Active and Passive Adaptivity

Agile management ensures that organizations are adaptive to changing requirements. In Section 3.2, we saw that changes can have two different causes.

Passive Adaptive

Changes can arise out of external developments such as market trends,
which can be analyzed via the STEEPLED model, and contribute to

Macro-level changes

Socio-cultural   Technology

Market changes

Updated products
or strategies   New
of competitors   entrants

Economy   Environment

**Internal
changes**

Structure
Processes
Systems
Changes in   Staffing   New
the strength or   Capabilities   substitutes
opportunities   Leadership
of suppliers   Culture
Political   (and their   Legal
                    suppliers)

Changing needs,
behaviour or power of customers
(and the 'customer's customer')

Ethical   Demographic

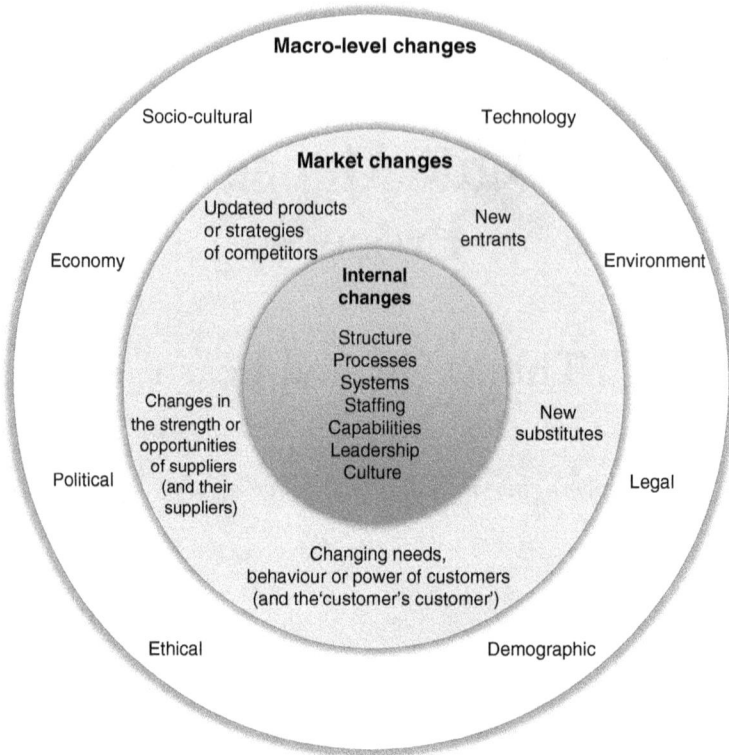

*Figure 9.1 Autonomous developments can take place externally and
internally*

changes in competitors and customers. Sometimes, these developments
are internal, such as changes in IT systems, staffing, skills, leadership, and
culture, which we analyze using the 7S model. The above is summarized
in Figure 9.1. If an organization adapts this way, they can be called *passive
adaptive*.

To be able to anticipate or react quickly and effectively, it is important
to periodically monitor the elements in Figure 9.1. For changes that fit
within its schema, it is necessary to determine what effects they might have
(or be having) on your organization. And finally, you need to estimate the
severity of their possible impact (high/medium/low) and the probability
(high/medium/low) that this will happen. This simple equation lets you
determine where you need to pay the most attention:

$$Priority = Impact \times Probability.$$

Active Adaptive

Alternatively, the change may be a result of an organization's own initiatives. Here we are talking about *active adaptivity*. This concerns the strategy you have chosen. You start with your market definition, and this serves as your compass. Your market definition is about your common purpose. It is a description of the market your organization focuses on. For example, does British Airways focus on transport in general or only by air? And only passengers, or cargo too? And only nationally, or internationally? Those choices have far-reaching consequences. For example, for what British Airways sees as its direct or indirect competitors, such as bus and train companies, car rental companies, shipping companies, and maybe even car manufacturers and tour operators. And for who British Airways considers as its potential customers, for example only consumers, or also business travelers. Overall, with a good and clear market definition, you have, as it were, ring-fenced your domain.

The adjustments that you make to your market definition and your go-to-market strategy are in-company initiatives that also lead to change. The initiatives that mostly occur can be seen in the Ansoff Matrix, Figure 9.2. These are:

- modifications to existing products or services in existing markets ("market penetration");
- introduction of new products or services in the current or new market ("proposition development" and "diversification");
- introduction of existing products or services in a new market ("market development").

Let us, for illustration, look at Starbucks. When Howard Schultz took over the company in 1987, there were six branches. Although coffee consumption had fallen, year on year for a decade, he noticed that the market for specialty coffee had increased from 3 to 10 percent in the same period. He decided to focus on affluent, highly educated people who had money for "gourmet" coffee. In addition, he wanted to create a "third place" where people could spend time in addition to the home and office. By 2013, Starbucks was established in sixty countries and sales

	Existing products/services	New products/services
Existing markets	**Market penetration** Customer development: increasing buying frequency, upselling and deep-selling of products/services	**Proposition development** Customer development: cross selling of extended, related or completely new products/services
New markets	**Market development** Approach customers of competitors, or in new markets or with minor adaptations to products/services	**Diversification** Horizontal, vertical or lateral development of new markets and/or products/services

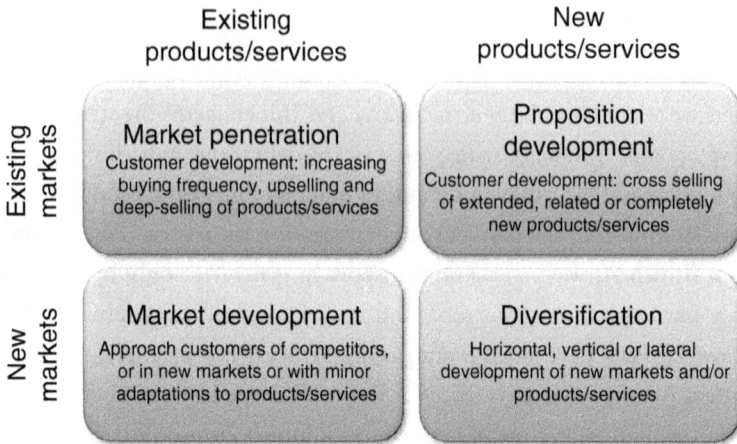

Figure 9.2 The Ansoff Matrix shows your strategic options

totaled $14.9 billion, with a gross profit of $2.5 billion. But this growth was not achieved without setbacks. In 2006, Starbucks were opening seven new stores a day but, in the crisis years between 2007 and 2010, the company had to close approximately 900 branches and lay off more than 34,000 workers.[1]

When the global economy recovered, growth returned, aided by a sophisticated strategy. Here is how that strategy might look through the lens of the Ansoff Matrix[2]:

- *Market penetration*—Starbucks wants to improve its products for its core customers. In a limited number of branches, it invests in the so-called Clover coffee machines and exclusive kinds of beans, which, together, produce superior coffee. Additionally, for all branches, they improve the entire range of "La Boulange" patisserie goods.
- *Proposition development*—Following the acquisition of the retail chain Teavana, which sells exclusive teas and tea accessories, Starbucks Coffee begins offering teas in all its branches. In addition, they increase their product range to include oatmeal cookies, nonalcoholic cocktails, and iced coffee.
- *Market development*—Starbucks accelerates the opening of offices abroad again, rolling out its international expansion.

- *Diversification*—Starbucks responds to the trend of health and wellness by opening Evolution Fresh branches, which also sell juices, salads, and wraps. They offer packaged Starbuck's coffee and beans in their own branches and also in third-party outlets.

About Red and Blue Oceans

In this situation, the Ansoff Matrix is a good tool that gives you an overview of your strategic options, which you can define and analyze. The attractiveness of these options can be determined by assessing the strength of suppliers, buyers, and competitors, as well as the threats of substitutes and new entrants using Porter's Five Forces model. Each of the five forces has multiple subfactors, but the full application of Porter's model is beyond the scope of this book (there are many good books and articles about it.).

However, it is worthwhile to stop for a moment and examine a particular aspect of diversification. In his excellent book *Blue Ocean Strategy*,[3] Chan Kim coined the terms "blue oceans" and "red oceans" as metaphors for the competitive field in which your company operates. The red ocean is a bloody place: filled with sharks, constantly fighting with each other for their piece of the prey. In the real world, this means that there are too many strong providers offering very similar products and services. In a saturated market, they can only compete on price to gain market share, creating a downward price-spiral. In the longer term, only a handful of players will remain, and all will need to minimize their costs repeatedly, to make any kind of profit. The choice for *operational excellence* is their only chance to survive. We all want to avoid swimming in a red ocean.

But a blue ocean is worth a plunge. We're not saying it's a subtropical swimming pool with a waterslide and a hot tub, but the blue ocean symbolizes the unknown market space—space that you create yourself instead of fighting competitors for it: you make the competition irrelevant. Instead of battling for a slice of the pie or the crumbs, you simply make the pie bigger. Just like a wedding cake, upon which you put another tier where you can eat all alone. Because everything in this additional market space is new, there are no rules yet, and that gives you opportunities that do not exist in the red ocean. You can maximize these opportunities by renewing or refreshing your product or service, so that you create value for both your customer and your own organization. In addition, you need to reduce costs for things that your clients find less important. The chance here is great that you can introduce a real *game changer*.

But where on the map can you find the blue ocean? I imagine that, sometimes, you go to the theatre; maybe you've even been to the circus. Both have their limitations. The theatre is usually static, auditoria are usually not that big, and the building is often in a relatively inaccessible location in the downtown area. The circus is especially fun for children, often a little corny, with a musty old tent and worn benches. And rather sad for the animals, right? Would you have thought of combining circus and theatre? That's exactly what, 30 years ago, the Cirque du Soleil did: creating a unique and very successful genre of entertainment, and they remain the only provider. They still use a tent, but theirs is beautiful, warm, large, and airy with very comfy chairs. There are no animals, but the acts are impressive, involving much color, light, movement, and live music. An impressing experience where you can spend a lot of money without a problem, entertaining your business partners or staff, and where you can also treat them to a superb dinner before the show. A brilliant business model: high prices and no competition.

Then there's Dyson, asking very high prices for powerful bagless vacuum cleaners with a nice design. And Swatch, who found a gap in the market for Swiss watches for a product with modern design and good quality at an affordable price. Or Nintendo, who changed gaming forever with its 3D dual touchscreen for its portable gaming machine and the motion sensor on its Wii console. Or else, the US do-it-yourself chain Home Depot, which sells very popular courses for budding handymen. And, of course, the hit show Starlight Express that really pushed the boundaries of the musical.

Overall, if you can, look at diversifying into a blue ocean. Grab your travel-sickness pills, stretch out your sea legs, put on your sou'wester, and step aboard the blue ocean reconnaissance ship.

New Requirements: Internal and External

Whether you adapt passively or actively, you are going to have to deal with new requirements; requirements that can be external or internal.

In both cases, this manifests concretely in the customer behavior. *External* is obviously the market: the people or institutions that buy your products or services. *Internal* means the departments within your own organization, your internal customers. As you saw in Section 7.2, the internal customer is always the next step in the value creation for the external customer. This step is represented by a process that arises from another (and in some cases your own) department. The output of one process is the input for the next; one process is always the customer of the preceding process. This is a fundamental principle of the Lean approach: *The next process is the customer.*

Now it's time to take some concrete steps, guided by the results of your STEEPLED or 7S analyses and the strategy you chose via the Ansoff matrix and Porter's Five Forces model. And that's precisely what agile management's *Think–Do–Learn* cycle is designed to help you do.

9.2   The Think–Do–Learn Cycle: The Basis of the Agile Management Process

As you now know, agile management is a way of working which, at its core, uses experimentation to achieve continuous learning and improvement. By working with hypotheses, minor adjustments are made in processes, products, services, or experiences. Then these are tested in practice and, on the basis of the results, adjustments are reversed, retained, further refined, or supplemented. This cycle continues indefinitely.

Many different variations of this cycle, with their own names, are in circulation. You might come across:

- the *build–measure–learn* cycle within the Lean Startup approach (and ING's *think–try–adjust* approach or the *try–listen–refine* approach of McDonald's);
- the *define–measure–analyze–improve–control* cycle or the *define–measure–analyze–design–verify* cycle within the Six Sigma approach;
- the *observe–orient–design–act* cycle in the Boyd decision-making process;
- the feedback cycle of *sprint* meetings within the Scrum approach.

Despite their differences, what all these cycles have in common is that they are based on the principles of the Plan–Do–Check–Act cycle, which—as we saw in Section 6.1—is, in its turn, based on the empirical cycle of the scientific method. The PDCA process is probably the most well-known and proven cycle because PDCA is central to the Toyota Production System and to Lean. Here's an example of how proven the PDCA cycle is: the US space agency NASA cannot afford to make any mistakes, and this applies especially to their complex cooperation with foreign organizations such as ESA, JAXA, CSA, and Roscosmos within the International Space Station project. That's why NASA applies the PDCA cycle in all its processes.

What is special about the PDCA cycle is that it can facilitate major breakthroughs, as well as frequent small improvements, in new and existing situations. This makes it suitable across innovation, product development, continuous improvement, and achieving adaptivity. For these reasons, the PDCA process was selected as the supporting platform for the principles of agile management. But, because experience showed that many organizations have difficulty distinguishing between the Check and Act phases, for practical considerations, we combined them. And in order to emphasize the goal of experimenting, we also changed the nomenclature here. Our resulting cycle has three steps, known as *Think, Do,* and *Learn.* Figure 9.3 is a global look at the content of the three continually repeating steps of the agile management process.

The better you are in the application of these process steps, the faster it will go, spinning your agile flywheel and making your organization continually more adaptive. See it as a vortex that makes a whirlpool shape in the water. The top of the vortex is wider than the bottom. The top circles, which you first go through, have a greater circumference than the circles that you go through later, at the bottom. If you maintain a constant speed, you'll go through the lower circles in a shorter time. So, the longer you work in the vortex of the agile management process, the more knowledge and experience you gain and the shorter the duration of each iteration.

To stay with the metaphor of a vortex, even the trunk of a tornado has this form. The speed of rotation gives a tornado its enormous sucking power. So the vortex of the *Think–Do–Learn* cycle gives your organization the power, as it were, to rapidly suck changes in and "process"

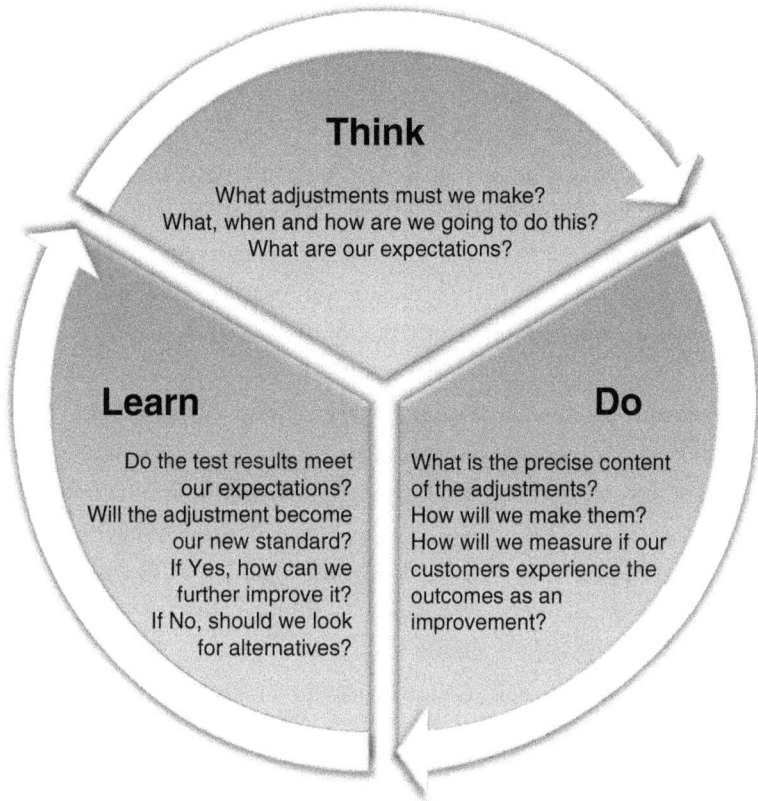

Think

What adjustments must we make?
What, when and how are we going to do this?
What are our expectations?

Learn

Do the test results meet
our expectations?
Will the adjustment become
our new standard?
If Yes, how can we
further improve it?
If No, should we look
for alternatives?

Do

What is the precise content
of the adjustments?
How will we make them?
How will we measure if our
customers experience the
outcomes as an
improvement?

Figure 9.3 The three steps within the agile management process

them. Incidentally, it is not true that the *Think–Do–Learn* cycle is a rigid
sequential process. This is truly iterative in nature. That means that sometimes you quickly go back and forth between the *Think* and *Do* phases,
because you have discovered something on the way that asks you to change
your assumptions. So you act quickly, responding on the basis of insights
gained.

In the sections that follow, we focus on the purpose and activities of
each of the three steps separately.

9.3 Think: Identifying and Prioritizing Improvements

During the *Think* phase, you determine what the goals will be for a new
iteration of the *Think–Do–Learn* cycle. These goals can be based on the
outcome of the *Learn* phase of your just-completed iteration. For example,

because a particular change in approach does not give rise to the expected improvements in the result. Or it does, so you're wondering what might deliver additional change. In both cases, you are curious about what has caused the just-completed iteration to meet or not meet expectations.

Of course you might start with something completely new, or you might be using the *Think–Do–Learn* cycle for the first time. Then, you cannot use the results of the *Learn* phase as your starting point, so you have to choose another. In this case, you can formulate your goals based on the "voice of the customer" sources, which form part of the *Learn* phase.

In both cases, it means that you are trying to discover what new requirements your organization must meet and how it can adapt to them in the best and quickest way. Making adaptivity tangible starts with setting good goals and adjusting to them. Apart from formulating these goals, during the *Think* phase, you will have to identify how you will achieve them concretely. In other words, you'll need to know who is going to do the work, and how and when.

For determining both targets and activities, you are lucky to have a box full of practical tools. Chapters 10 and 11, therefore, examine the following instruments:

- Business-model canvas;
- Value-stream mapping and process mapping;
- Personas and customer journeys;
- Prioritizing activities;
- Working with hypotheses and metrics;
- Flexible planning.

9.4   Do: Building and Testing Improvements

Once you've completed the *Think* phase, you are ready for the next step: *Do*. Here you are going to carry out those activities to which you have given the highest priority, in two steps. Whatever you plan to adapt and adjust, you first have to build. This could be something very small or something very big. For example, it could be just the customization of a particular phone number, or the launch of a completely new product. And because, at its best, agile management works as much as possible in small steps, that large project for the launch of a new product can be cut down into as many small projects as practical. However you approach things, you will always have building activities. Second, you should offer what you've built to your internal or external customer to find out how he reacts: *The proof of the pudding is in the eating*. So you will need to conduct measurements to determine whether your expectations, that you set as hypotheses during the *Think* phase, are actually true.

To do this effectively, there's a doctor's bag full of handy instruments just for this. In Chapter 12, the following are discussed:

- Building customer-value propositions;
- Building customer experiences;
- The "minimum viable product";
- Testing and measuring.

9.5   Learn: What Have the Improvements Delivered?

All the activities are now behind you and all the measurements have been completed: time to determine how the *Do* phase went. Now you want to know to what degree the test results you have measured match your expectations. You also want to determine to what extent the implementation of activities in the *Do* phase went according to plan. Are there any notable exceptions? To what extent was your plan correct and complete in order to best facilitate the implementation?

The *Learn* phase is about gathering as much relevant information as possible about what happened during the *Do* phase. To this end, many different sources are available. Besides measuring your own activities, you will especially need to look at the behavior of your internal or external customer. How did he react to the adjustments you made?

Once this information is complete, you can determine whether the adjustments that you experimented with, during the *Do* stage, have brought an improvement compared with the previous approach (also known as the standard or baseline). If so, then this is the new standard and, naturally, you will be curious to learn if there is further room for improvement. If not, this will remain the current standard and you can look for possible alternatives, or get started with all the other changes from your prioritized to-do list. In every case, there is still something to learn, which means that you can start a new iteration of the *Think–Do–Learn* cycle.

In order to make optimal use of the *Learn* phase, another arsenal full of weapons and ammunition is at your disposal. These are discussed in Chapter 13:

- Evaluation
- "Voice of the customer" sources
- Pivoting and continuing

In short, get to work! For how to make a useful start, see Chapter 10.

By reading this chapter, you'll have discovered the following:
- *You can be either passive adaptive or active adaptive. Passive means that you monitor the internal and external changes and you adjust to them. Active means that you take the initiative, within the framework of the Ansoff Matrix, and that these initiatives require adjustments.*
- *To facilitate these adjustments, in addition to how the organization is structured, is another foundation-stone of the agile management approach: the process. This process is a cycle based on the scientific method. The process consists of three steps: Think, Do, and Learn.*
- *In the Think phase, you determine what improvement possibilities exist and which have priority. The Do phase sees you building and testing your improvements. The Learn phase is about seeing what your improvements have delivered and, based on these results, what the next logical step should be.*

References

1. Loeb, L. (2013). "Starbucks: Global Coffee Giant has New Growth Plans." *Forbes*. January 31.
2. Gertner, J. (2012). "Most Innovative Companies in 2012: 24–Starbucks." *Fast Company*, February 7.
3. Kim, C., and R. Mauborgne. (2005). *Blue Ocean Strategy*. Brighton: Harvard Business School Press.

CHAPTER 10

The Think Phase—Discover How You can Excel

Imagination is more important than knowledge.
For knowledge is limited, whereas imagination embraces the
entire world, stimulating progress, giving birth to evolution.
—Albert Einstein

In this first chapter covering the first step in the agile management process, the *Think* phase, you will see how to translate new requirements into concrete results. You'll also learn how to determine what improvements you want to experiment with in the next iteration of the *Think–Do–Learn* cycle. Among others, we'll be looking at these subjects.

10.1   Working with the Business Model Canvas

Each of the changes which you read about in section 9.1 has a direct impact on your business model. And you'll have to adapt your business model to these new requirements. Much of this approach uses the *Business Model Canvas (BMC)*, which, in turn, often illustrates issues using the 80/20 rule, which we encountered in section 6.1. The canvas gives your team a format to brainstorm and design in an iterative way, making a practical and, importantly, visual outline of your ideas. Ideas that might relate to entirely new products or services, but also to adapting and improving existing products and services. The BMC's speed and flexibility, and the fact that the approach suits both internal and external customers, makes it ideal for agile management. Based on the words and images of the canvas you create, you can break these down into detailed parts and then experiment to find out what does and does not work well in practice.

An Example: Apple

When Steve Jobs returns to Apple, in the late 90s, the company is on its last legs. He recognizes that innovation is the only way to save his "baby," and one of his first steps is to introduce the iPod.

Figure 10.1 shows you an overview, in BMC format,[1] of the *canvas* for the iPod that Apple launched in 2001. At this time, the market is full of competitive MP3 players. For users, however, it is difficult to convert their existing music collections into MP3 format for these players. Also transferring their music files to the player is complicated and time consuming. Moreover, the players cannot display details of the music in a simple, easy-to-understand way. And, finally, there is almost no music available for online purchase and download, as music companies can only imagine negative consequences from this kind of

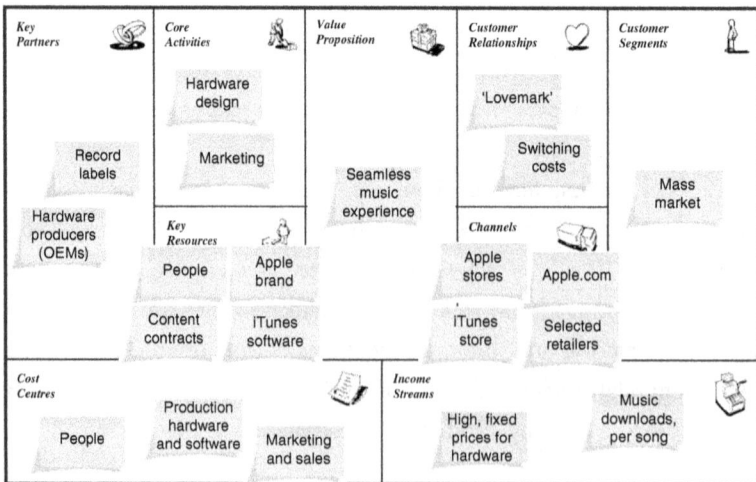

Figure 10.1 The business model canvas for Apple's iPod

sales model and are unwilling to work together. This is partly because, at this time, a lot of music is being illegally downloaded from sites like Napster.

Apple sees a great opportunity for offering a seamless music experience. Hardware and software must work together in a very user-friendly way and the artists' music must be organized and accessible, in a single location, and be easy to buy and get onto your own player or computer. It should be an experience with which everyone will fall in love. At the same time, it happens that the choice of an iPod and iTunes, and the time and money that users invest in building their music collections, ensures they never want to switch to future competitors. Apple generates massive revenues through smart channel-management. The hardware is sold via its own channels and through selected retailers, and high prices are set and maintained.

Hardware, software, and content go hand-in-hand. After the launch, Apple goes to work customizing the experience by making significant, step-by-step improvements. In addition to repeated small improvement steps, Apple is also taking giant steps. In 2003, it launches the iTunes Store, designed to be an integral part of the iTunes software experience. Exclusive agreements with almost all music companies ensure that competitors cannot easily enter this market. The iTunes store offers a very low entry point, with single numbers selling at only $0.99. Payment is quick and easy via an iTunes account and the download begins immediately, taking only a few moments. Gradually, Apple broadens its content offerings, adding podcasts and video.

In 2007, Apple then takes a massive step: from the iPod, it creates the iPhone and brings it to market. As we saw in Chapter 2, this is ultimately the final blow for market leaders Nokia and BlackBerry. It is a *game changer*, a totally disruptive technology. A revolutionary device with graphical touch screen operation, which works seamlessly with iTunes for music and software updates and adds a new word to our dictionaries: *smartphone*. Apple creates incredible interest, and consumers are rushing to pay Apple's high prices. The same year sees the launch of the Apple TV, which works with iTunes on existing televisions and computers including Window's PCs. Improvement never falters and, step by regular step, Apple adds and updates features and services.

In 2008, within an update to the iTunes program, Apple launches the App Store. For iPhone users, it offers Apple-approved games, and apps from non-Apple developers, both free and paid. The revenue model guarantees Apple 30 percent of all sales generated by an app. By enforcing developer standards that ensure seamless working between hardware, software, and content, Apple distinguishes itself from the fragmented supply models of all the other smartphone brands and app stores.

Another giant step occurs in 2010, when Apple is again a *first mover* with the introduction of a tablet, the iPad. Similar to the iPhone, it functions seamlessly with iTunes and the App Store. The tablet offers a brand new app, the Apple iBook, for the purchase and reading of e-books: Apple is now a direct competitor of Amazon and other e-book and e-reader providers.

In 2015, Apple launched its subscription service for streaming music, Apple Music. It does so to address the decline in iTunes music sales resulting from the success of Spotify.

By the end of 2016, Apple has sold a total of 1,023 billion iPhones, 338 million iPads, and, by the end of 2015, 404 million iPods and 26 million Apple TVs—nearly 1.8 billion units in total. iTunes and the App Store have approximately 575 million customers, who have downloaded a total of 45 billion songs, 6 billion videos, and 100 billion apps. There are 43 million songs, 240,000 movies and TV shows, and 1.4 million apps available.[2]

Now that we have explored how one uses the canvas, via the iPod example, we can go look, in a little more detail, at the different parts of the canvas.

Right Section = Value

The canvas consists of fields with very close relationships. It facilitates your adaptivity, because changes can be made visible within the *Customer segments* field at the top right. In it, you describe what requirements your target group—whether it is an internal customer within your own organization or external in the market—demands from your organization, department, or team. This also applies to the *Channels* field: here you describe which channels your internal/external customer wants to use in relation to your products and services. Through these you detail, as precisely as possible, what the customer wants and how you can best deliver it. Paragraphs 10.3 and 10.4 display this analysis in the form of the *persona* and *customer journey*.

The requirements of your target audience are the basis for the central field, the *Value proposition*. Here, you translate the desires and needs of the internal or external customer to the features and benefits of your products and services. You translate them in relationship to how you (as you described in the *Customer relationships* field) want to engage with customers and how this should generate revenue (as in the *Revenue streams* field). How this process will work exactly, is discussed in section 12.1.

This right section, made up of the five fields; *Customer segments, Channels, Value proposition, Customer relationships,* and *Revenue streams,* forms the core of the BMC. This is where value is created; it is the hub around which the rest revolves.

Left Section = Effectiveness and Efficiency

The remaining four parts in the left section are based on those on the right side and focus on effectiveness and efficiency. Which of the *Key activities, Key resources,* and *Key partners* are needed to make this possible? And which *Cost structures* belong with them? Changes in the five core areas above have direct consequences for the other four areas, because they must be adjusted accordingly. This is a concrete example of adaptivity in practice. It helps to ask yourself certain questions while using the 80/20 rule, and you can find these in Table 10.1.

This book focuses on the right side of the canvas and will not elaborate on the *Key activities, Key resources, Key partners,* and *Cost structures.* For those interested, details, explanations, and examples can be found in the excellent book *Business Model Generation* by Osterwalder and Pigneur. However, it is worth staying for the next section, covering methods to analyze and optimize the left section of the canvas. These are *value-stream mapping* and *process mapping*.

Table 10.1 The translation of the right to the left side of the canvas

Fields of the Business Model Canvas	Questions that help adapt to changes in customer segments, channels, value propositions, and customer relationships
Key activities	• Which (changes in our) activities are required by our value proposition, channels, customer relationships, and revenue streams? • How do we design (or adapt) our processes for these changes? • What (change in) performance should the new processes deliver? • How will we measure and analyze the activities and performance?

Key resources	• How do we focus our organization to effectively and efficiently carry out our key activities?
	• What resources are required to perform our key activities:
	  ○ natural resources (e.g., energy, water, raw materials)
	  ○ semifinished products and packaging
	  ○ production facilities (e.g., buildings, machinery and vehicles)
	  ○ offices and workplaces
	  ○ IT systems (e.g., hardware, software and networks)
	  ○ people
	  ○ legal agreements and intellectual property (e.g., permits, contracts, patents, and trademarks)
	  ○ financial instruments (e.g., cash, loans, options, equities, and insurance).

Key partners	• Which suppliers do we need to deliver our value proposition? This involves all the key resources above. • Which partners do we need for our distribution network? E.g., transportation, storage, and sales (importers, wholesalers, retailers) • What specialists do we need to support our processes? E.g., recruitment, marketing, IT, legal, accountancy
Cost structures	• What are the main fixed and variable costs related to our key activities, key resources, and key partners? • What and where should we invest? • Are there economies of scale and scope that will be beneficial?

10.2 Internal Perspective: Value-Stream Mapping and Process Mapping

Value-stream mapping and *process mapping* have their origins in the Toyota Production System and Lean (as discussed in chapter 6). These methods suit all types of organizations in all industries, whether production or services, profit or nonprofit, business or consumer markets, digital or physical processes. You can use them from two perspectives: first to dig deeper into the BMC as discussed above; second, they can be used separately from the canvas. For example, because you find that you have a limited grasp of why your internal processes don't seem to be going very well and are hindering value creation. Often, then, internal customers are complaining about their internal suppliers. Or you observe symptoms via other sources, such as indicators, abnormalities, incidents, ideas, audits, risk assessments, and inquiries.

Value-stream mapping allows you to analyze multiple processes simultaneously. These processes can be synchronous or sequential. What you're looking for is whether the possibility exists to achieve improvements *between* these processes. Process mapping means you choose a specific process and look *within* it to see what might be improved.

Become a Garbage-Collector

Both approaches are about identifying where value can be created for internal or external customers. Value is anything for which the customer is willing to pay, literally or figuratively. Naturally you want to get the most out the process of value creation. To achieve this, you might try imagining yourself as a kind of garbage-collector, walking along behind a garbage truck that's cruising through your organization and picking up waste wherever you encounter it. By "waste" (what Lean calls *muda*), we mean any affairs or activities that do not add value, or which impose an unnecessary burden on your resources. This involves the flow of information, services, and goods throughout the organization.

Often, looking at abstract figures in reports can give you an incomplete or distorted view of these issues. The best way to learn what is needed is to get out from behind your desk and start investigating. See for yourself how things are really going in your contact centers, shops, offices, factory, or department. That is where it is happening. Lean knows this as the principle of *genchi gembutsu*.

But in which garbage bags are you going to start looking? There are nine different kinds:

1. *Overproduction*—If too much is produced, too quickly for the internal or external customer's demand, this unnecessarily uses

raw materials, part-finished goods, personnel, and equipment. It also creates unnecessary transport, storage, and administration and consumes funds.

2. *Stock*—Above a certain minimum level (*just-in-time*), stockpiling puts an unnecessary burden on resources such as buildings, transport, staff, administration, and finance. The organization also then runs the risk of theft, fire, as well as quality reduction, and value loss due to aging.

3. *Defects*—Products and services that have errors or defects provide additional work and costs because things need to be fixed. They might even need to be destroyed, meaning totally writing-off all the time, money, and resources that went into their production.

4. *Movement*—If employees need to make unnecessary movements when handling or operating devices or servicing clients, it will cost unnecessary time and energy. Think of a service-counter employee who constantly has to walk back and forth to the printer or to a storeroom to get brochures and cards.

5. *Process design*—Are processes logically designed? If not, then this leads to waste within the work itself. Consider the process of mortgage-application processing, which almost always proceeds sequentially, while many steps can be executed in parallel. Or a process which has unnecessary steps. Such as when a customer fills out a web form, which an employee then prints and sends to a colleague, who manually copies this into a quotation, which is then emailed back to the customer, and then printed and stored for reference during follow-up calls.

6. *Waiting times*—Employees sitting still, because they can't do anything, is a waste of time. This happens, for example, when they have to wait for information from a system or from a colleague. Or if parts are missing, equipment isn't working, or the employee is simply overseeing a colleague (or device) who is performing value-adding activities.

7. *Transport*—Unnecessary handling of materials can result from overproduction or unnecessary inventory. Products can also be transported unnecessarily due to less-than-optimal routing in the distribution network, or information travelling horizontally or vertically, via too many people, before arriving at the person who needs it.

8. *Wasted time*—This applies when employees are unnecessarily using time. For example, when they seek clarification about a poorly explained task. Or when they must search, sort, correct, interrupt, find inaccessible colleagues, participate in irrelevant meetings, monitor the progress of complex processes, and so on.

9. *Instability*—In addition, it is possible that your processes are unstable (Lean calls this *mura*). There are too many peaks and troughs in the speed and magnitude of the flow of information, services, and products. In other words, it's all or nothing, causing your processes to deteriorate in quality and efficiency. Think of how busy it can be in shops or contact centers during particular seasons, holidays, or at weekends. You must have the capacity for these peak times, but avoid unnecessary costs in the quiet times, while you always want to deliver a quality experience.

Visualizing

When you have been in the workplace, it can be helpful, later, to visualize what you found. This helps you to organize your own thoughts or to engage others in identifying opportunities for improvements. With brown paper*, sticky notes, and markers, you can represent the current progress of a particular process or group of processes for a specific product or service. While drawing and looking at the result, you often discover how things could be improved. Figure 10.2 shows a simplified example of a *process map* for the repair of lease cars.

For example, in mapping out the above process, it was discovered that customers were often unpleasantly surprised to learn they had to pay a part of the cost; their *excess* or *own risk*. This was because customers were not always informed about the consequences of choosing for a nonapproved bodyshop in place of one approved by the lease/insurance company. In addition, there could be significant possible savings in processing time, by allowing customers to make direct contact with the bodyshop instead of through the leasing company.

---

*The Dutch business community regularly uses large-sized rolls of brown wrapping paper for this purpose.

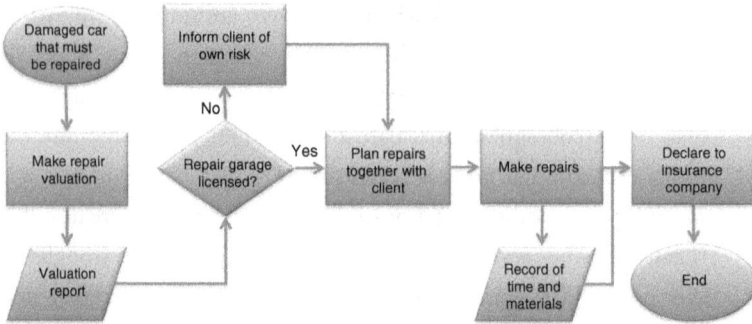

Figure 10.2 Process map for car repair

10.3   The Persona: Your Customer as Imaginary Friend

Now that we have discussed the internal perspective, in 10.2, it is time to use the BMC to examine the external perspective. As we saw in the first two of the eight agile principles, the organization should operate with an outside-in perspective rather than inside-out. For long, many organizations thought that they were the center of the universe, with customers circling around them. But actually, it is the opposite: the customer is in the middle and is free to choose with which of the multiple organizations circling around him he will spend his money. Just as Copernicus, contrary to popular belief, found out that earth was orbiting the sun.

So organizations should be customer-centric. This requires, among other things, to get into the customer's head; into his desires, needs, and behavior. This applies both to internal and external customers. For this, you can use the *voice of the customer* information sources that you'll see later in section 13.2.

From Market Definition to Market Segmentation

It is easy to identify your internal customers, but not so easy, perhaps, with external customers. So let's look at the latter. In Section 9.1, you already saw how you define your market. The next step is to determine which segments you believe make up your market. A segment is a group of (potential) customers with common characteristics, which is distinctly different from another group. You could say segments are internally homogeneous and mutually heterogeneous. But how do you establish what your segments are? Via segmentation criteria.

So segmentation criteria address the features of (potential) customers and come in three "flavors":

1. Socio-demographic factors: what are they?
   - These are hard criteria such as residential address, age, gender, education, income, and family situation.
   - For business markets this is called *firmographics*, and includes data such as the business address, turnover, number of employees, industry type, and DMU (*decision-making unit*: roles, for example, such as buyer, user, influencer, and decision maker).
2. Behavior: what do they do?
   - First, how do they use the product or service? Consider the type of product or service, response, importance to the user, when used, how often, where, how—and how much/often—is it used, degree of loyalty, how long as a customer and status (active, dormant, prospect).
   - In addition, you can look at how they use orientation channels, sales channels, and usage channels.
   - Online channels offer the advantage of being able to perform real-time segmentation by looking at click behavior (for instance, with the help of cookies).
3. Attitude: what do they think and feel?
   - This concerns soft criteria such as beliefs, motivations, desires, needs and goals, preferences, buying motives, and criteria (*unique buying reasons*), attitudes toward specific topics and products/services, willingness to adopt innovations, and who or what influences them (e.g., media, authorities, communities, colleagues, stakeholders, references, examples).

By defining which segmentation criteria are relevant to you and combining them with each other, you try to form unique groups. Think of it as the well-known board game *Who is it?*, where you have to guess an opponent's "person" by asking Yes/No questions about their characteristics. Similar to how you find your ideal partner on a dating site. So diagnose like a doctor: you ask ever-deeper logical questions until you have a clear picture. A useful tool is the *nested approach (see* Figure 10.3*)*, originally developed by Bonoma and Shapiro for business markets, but also well suited to consumer markets. In this model, you work from the outside to the inside.

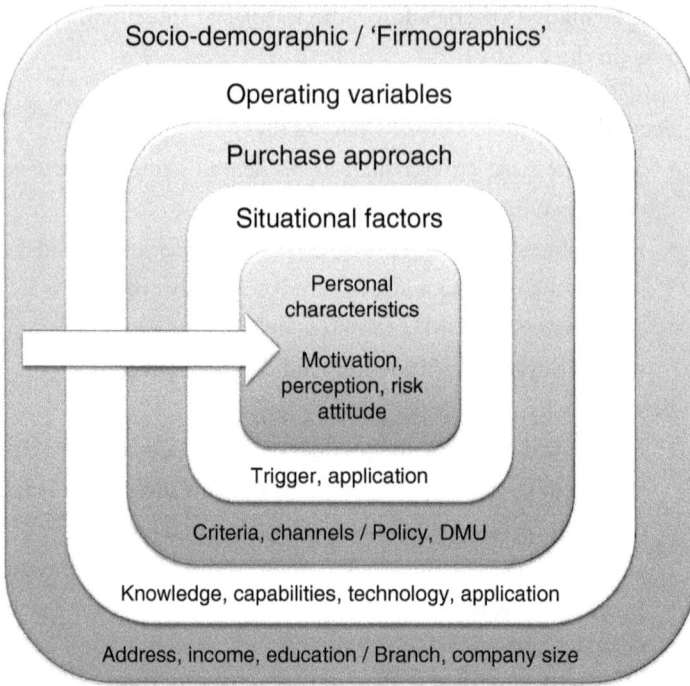

Figure 10.3 The "nested approach"; at the bottom are examples of criteria for the related step

So you start with hard criteria, which are usually the easiest, and then you see how much further you can get using progressively softer criteria.

You'll also need to be sure that the criteria are traceable. In other words, you have to be able to designate specific people or companies, within a market segment, from your desk. (And, for example, this might be difficult if you segment by people with curly hair and blue eyes). Sometimes, it can be useful to look for a so-called *proxy*, a criterion which can be an indicator of what you are looking for. For example, in consumer markets, the postcode is a reliable indicator of criteria such as income, education, and family situation.

How does this segmentation look in practice? In the leisure travel market, for example, you can distinguish between five segments:

1. *Planners*: older people with high incomes who spend a lot of money on package holidays. They book well in advance and often still use travel agencies and travel guides.

2. *Active holidaymakers*: older people with high incomes who spend a lot of money on long-distance travel or camping and hiking and are then active, at their holiday location, for example on tours and museum visits. They put their whole trip together themselves.
3. *Fun seekers*: young people who book impulsively. Mostly, they go to party islands, where they spend a lot of money on adventure activities, amusement parks, and clubs.
4. *Package buyers*: young people with a limited budget who book last-minute cheap package holidays.
5. *Stay-at-homes*: young families and young people living alone. They would rather spend their money on home-improvements or a car, and therefore they holiday in their own country, sometimes just making day trips.

From Market Segments to Target-Group Segments

When you have defined the market segments, the next question is which are you going to target. Some will be more attractive than others. This is called target-group selection. It entails scoring and then prioritizing your market segments based on two factors: the value, and chance of success. The value lies in aspects such as spending, potential gross margin, loyalty, and operating costs. Chances of success are about the *share of wallet*, references, access to decision makers, competitive pressures, and so on.

An example; for security companies, it is smart to focus on "triggers" as a selection criterion. If there have been recent break-ins to individuals or companies in their immediate environment, they are more likely to want to invest in an alarm system. So they constitute the primary target-group segment.

From Target-group Segments to Personas

Once you've selected your target-group segment(s) from the market segments, it can be very useful to develop a "persona." This concept dates back to the Roman times. A persona was a theatrical mask used by actors on stage to make immediately clear to the public what role they played. That mask had to be very recognizable. The same principle applies to organizations and their clients. Many people find it difficult, on the basis of a combination of abstract segmentation criteria, to get a clear idea or a concrete picture of the type of customer for whom they work (and who actually pays their salaries). And this hinders their customer focus and creativity. Therefore, it is smart to bring the customer to life by drawing a recognizable picture of his or her personality. As so often, this applies to both internal and external customers.

Look at it this way. Suppose you've bought a house and you've asked an interior designer to suggest a design for the rebuild. If he has already created a plan, he will walk with you through the house telling you what he has in mind in each area. He might suggest removing a wall, putting in glass doors, laying a wooden floor, or using a specific color of paint. After just a room or two, you might be finding him a bit difficult to follow, because most people are not very able to visualize something. And this is why many architects use special three-dimensional software to show their design to you. And then suddenly the penny drops. You will be excited (or not), begin thinking of other improvements and where you might start looking for new furniture.

And that is how it works with a persona. A persona is an archetype, a profile of a person—based on the 80/20 rule—that is a true representative of your target audience: a typical example or model, your quintessential customer. But how do you then define a persona? To do this you have to stand, empathetically, in the customer's shoes; try to *feel* what the customer feels. The starting point is obviously that you need to know as much as possible about the desires and needs of your target group's behavior. You can find more information about this, the *voice of the customer*, discussed in Chapter 12. If you lack any information, you can use assumptions, as long as you explicitly state this and validate their accuracy later. On this basis, you can describe your persona. You do that as a caricature, a stereotype. So the characteristics must stand out. A bit like the way children do when they are playing at being a policeman, fireman, knight, pilot, race-car driver, cook, flight-attendant or princess, or if they describe their imaginary boyfriend or girlfriend in detail. This facilitates persona recognition. Brings the customer to life. Here's an example:

You can use the Figure 10.4 format with your team in a workshop. You brainstorm by putting the headings on a whiteboard or blank paper and filling the areas in with sticky notes. You describe a persona always in relation to what your organization has to offer in the marketplace. In consumer markets you focus on one person. In business markets, preferably you do this too. But it might be that, given the importance of

TOM the TECH

A young professional
Tom is 35 years old and gained his degree via evening school. He loves working and has a passion for technology but, above all, a passion for quality. His skills, speed and flexibility have earned him some very loyal customers. Home electrics are his passion.

Quality first
Formerly Tom was employed, but is now a freelancer. He tales a very innovative approach to his work. He thinks along with his clients, advising them professionally and experimenting actively with original solutions. He truly enjoys fine craftsmanship. He does his own maintenance, and takes pleasure in solving complex problems.

Competition from handymen
Tom's fear is that he will fall behind the increasingly rapid technological advances because he hasn't enough time for the study needed to keep up-to-date. In addition, he is coming under increasing pressure from customers who confront him with online handymen offering lower hourly rates and cheaper products. These people only look at the short term and don't see the value in Tom. He suffers because he only recommends services and products in which he really believes, rather than cheap options for bigger profits.

Would like support
For Tom, money is not the most important thing. He likes doing his work, but hates all the paperwork that comes with being an entrepreneur. He would like to get affordable help.

Tom is very curious and prefers self-study. But he finds much of the available training too superficial and seeks more depth. He would also like to think along with his suppliers about innovative new products. Beautiful tools are too expensive a hobby, so he would like to be sponsored by a technical wholesaler or tool brand.

Figure 10.4 The persona of an electrician

the DMU, you need to describe an extra person for this role. Again, you can use the segmentation criteria that we discussed earlier:

- Who is it? Socio-demographic characteristics, such as age.
- What's he doing? What customer tasks, relevant to your organization should he perform?
- What does he feel? What rational and emotional outcomes and/ or benefits will the customer derive from his tasks? What are the undesirable results, and the risks and barriers to a positive customer experience, that accompany his performing the client tasks?

After the brainstorming, you should "challenge" the outcomes. You propose questions such as: Is the persona familiar to anyone? What is its essence? Can anyone give a concrete example of such a client in our practice? On what information is the persona based? Are there assumptions we have to validate? To what extent can the features described be recognized, for example, by our CRM system?

Where necessary, you refine the descriptions. You then add a fictitious name with a profile picture, possibly with an empathetic quote and *mood-board* images. Finally, you process the whole into a visual profile, as shown in Figure 10.4. It is a good idea, as much as possible, to communicate the persona daily within your organization, so that every employee is encouraged to think about how to do something better every day for the customer. You can put up posters, photo frames or, if you think they'll work, 3-D printed dolls. And come back to the persona again and again in conversations, meetings, emails, and presentations. The customer as icon, mascot, or pet.

10.4   Customer Journey: On Expedition with Your Customer

Based on your persona, you can start looking at customer behavior: what channels does the customer use, and when and for what purpose? And how does he feel about that; now? For this, we use a technique called *customer journey mapping*. Literally creating a map of the customer's journey. As you did with the *persona,* here you can again use the *voice of the customer,* supplemented, where necessary, with (to be) validated assumptions.

How does that work? You start by zooming in on the customer's tasks. A *customer job* (which is the official Lean terminology) consists of a set of activities performed by the customer with a specific goal in mind. Imagine someone who has just had his bike stolen. This is the trigger for the start of a process he, as a customer, will go through. He needs to buy another bike. How this is actually done, you can capture on brown paper while brainstorming with your team: what are steps he goes through and what customer tasks must he perform there? This leads to a list as shown in Figure 10.5.

From this list, you then select a *customer job,* in order to delve deeper into the customer journey. Let's do that now for the client task "*Seek advice.*" On fresh brown paper, you create three horizontal "swimming" lanes. In the middle, you describe the customer's behavior: what activities does the customer perform? Then you describe in the top lane where such activities take place, the *touchpoints.* And then comes the most important part: in the lower lane, for each activity and its *touchpoint,* you imagine what the customer experience is: positive, negative, or neutral. When the customer has a very strong experience, also called a *moment of truth,* you mark that, for example with a star (because here you have to shine as an organization). This leads to an overview as shown in Figure 10.6.

Persona: Bill Budget – Current process: cycle purchase and use					
Getting interested	Getting informed	Comparing	Choosing	Buying	Using
Sees bikes in ads and on the street	Seeks advice	Checks-out reviews	Sets features list	Negotiates price	Collects bike
Asks around his personal network	Finds and studies information	Creates a preference list	Makes definitive choice	Places order	Performs final check
Sets his budget		Compares prices			Buys accessories
					Carries out repairs

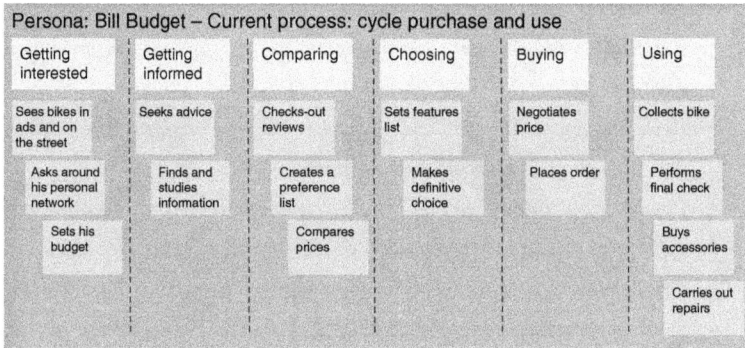

Figure 10.5 *The current customer process for the persona, "Bill Budget," for the purchase and use of a bicycle*

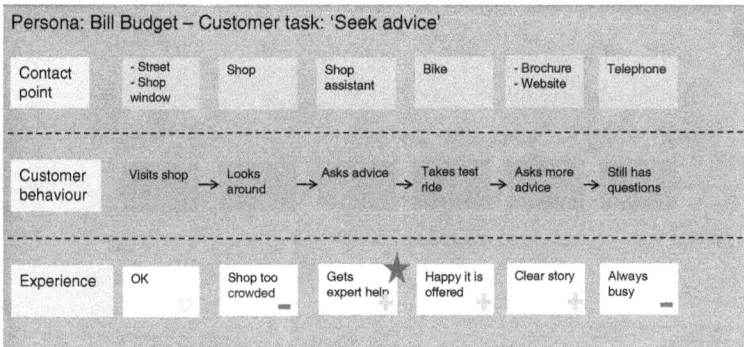

Persona: Bill Budget – Customer task: 'Seek advice'							
Contact point	- Street - Shop window	Shop	Shop assistant	Bike	- Brochure - Website	Telephone	
Customer behaviour	Visits shop	Looks around	Asks advice	Takes test ride	Asks more advice	Still has questions	
Experience	OK	Shop too crowded	Gets expert help	Happy it is offered	Clear story	Always busy	

Figure 10.6 *The customer journey analysis to seek advice when buying a bike*

A customer journey analysis works for both internal and external customers. It gives you direct insight into the opportunities for improvement; what and where they are. But which opportunity should you choose to start with? There is more about that in the next chapter.

By reading this chapter, you'll have discovered the following:

- *The Think phase is as short as possible; the focus should be on the Do phase.*
- *The Think phase usually comes down to prioritizing and planning, because from the existing to-do list, and new ideas from the Do and Learn phases, it is very clear what should be done (see Chapter 11).*

But for large projects, and organizations working for the first time with agile management, it is necessary to first make a comprehensive diagnosis.

- *Agile management works with "sketches" instead of plans. The Business Model Canvas is a useful starting point.*
- *On the right side of the canvas, the customer is central. To serve him optimally, you have to know who your customer is, what he wants, and what he does. Based on information gained during the* Learn *phase, you can use analysis methods such as the persona and customer journey.*
- *All this is applies to internal and external customers.*

References

1. Osterwalder, A., and Y. Pigneur. (2009*). Business Model Generation.* Netherlands: Wolters Kluwer.
2. Statista.com and wikipedia.org.

CHAPTER 11

The Think Phase—Create a Flexible Plan

Plans are worthless, but planning is everything.
—Dwight Eisenhower

In this second chapter about the *Think* phase, you'll learn a smart way to identify which improvement opportunities you should begin with in the next iteration. It looks at questions such as: Which improvements will have the most impact? Which costs the greatest effort? How do you make the efforts and results measurable? And how do we plan for all this?

11.1   Prioritizing Improvements

For organizations already comfortable working with agile management, the *Think* phase is usually short. Then the results of the *Do* and *Learn* phases usually give a very clear picture of what the next logical step is in a new iteration of the *Think–Do–Learn* cycle. During these phases, all the ideas for improvements are already on the existing to-do list. The *Think* phase is all about getting your priorities right. Moreover, as you already saw in section 3.1, markets are showing increased levels of VUCA: Volatility, Uncertainty, Complexity, and Ambiguity. This brings the organization's planning horizon much nearer, with the result that the effectiveness of developing large plans continues to decline, especially for the medium and long term. More and more organizations, therefore, choose to work on ideas and projects they can realize in the short term.

Such programs can be adapted faster when new insights are available. Emphasis here is on the *Do* phase.

Look at Impact and Effort

In Chapter 10, you read how, in the first part of the Think phase, you identify what opportunities for improvement exist. Unfortunately, though, resources such as time and money are scarce. You simply cannot do everything you want, and that's why you must constantly make choices regarding the activities that you will and will not perform. To make these choices, you first find out what the improvements will deliver and at what cost. Basically, you're going to prioritize based on the impact and the effort of each activity. It is best to work this out on a wall, whiteboard, or brown paper, using a two-by-two matrix with an axis of high/low impact versus an axis of high/low-effort (see Figure 11.1).

As Figure 11.1 shows, you can plot your improvements on the matrix. This can be done globally, while the S/M/L/XL classification makes further refinement possible. Improvements in the top left quadrant have the highest priority, then those in the bottom left quadrant, and then the top right. The improvements in the bottom right quadrant, you can forget, unless you really have nothing else to do. The question now is the

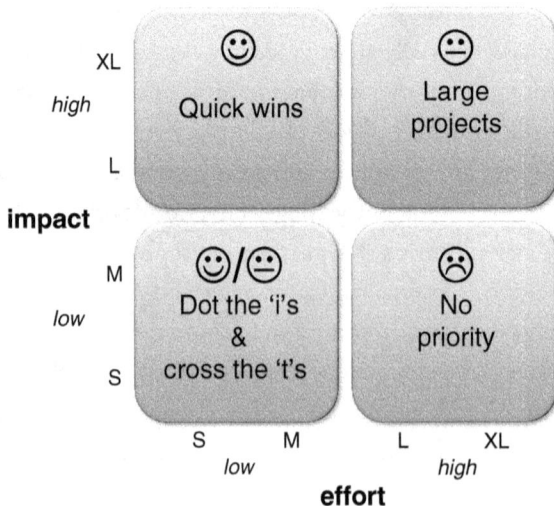

Figure 11.1 The impact–effort matrix

actual meaning of *impact* and *effort*. This is entirely dependent on your specific situation, and so you must formulate your own criteria.

From an *internal* perspective, a major impact might be to reduce waste (see section 10.2), which will produce cost savings. Another might be internal customer satisfaction. From an *external* perspective, for governments or nonprofit organizations, it concerns customer satisfaction of the external customers. This customer satisfaction is determined by both the expectations and the perceived experience of the customer, regarding the products, services, and channels. Consider, for example, the speed and quality of information, the usefulness of information, or the quality of a product (the SERVQUAL model is a useful tool here[1]; try Googling it).

For external customers of *commercial* organizations, it is about the impact, besides customer satisfaction, on value to the customer and the customer value: the amount of value you create for a client and, as a result, how much you can earn from him as long as this customer stays with you (Figure 11.2 presents this as a useful tree diagram). Customer value also includes cost savings. Incidentally, customer satisfaction has a strong influence on customer value, in particular the duration of the customer relationship, and the contribution to margin contained within that. Satisfied customers generally stay longer and spend more.[2]

Besides the impact, of course, there was the effort. Effort breaks down into issues such as:

- investments and costs;
- time use;
- lead time;
- systems use;
- opportunity costs (the revenue lost by not using your scarce resources for the best possible alternative activity);
- risks.

Now that your improvements are prioritized based on impact and effort, you can write each improvement on a Post-It and stick them, one under the other, in order of priority, on your brown paper. You've just made your first visual list, your first *product backlog*. Congratulations. According to Lean's *pull* principle, the team can now take the improvements on

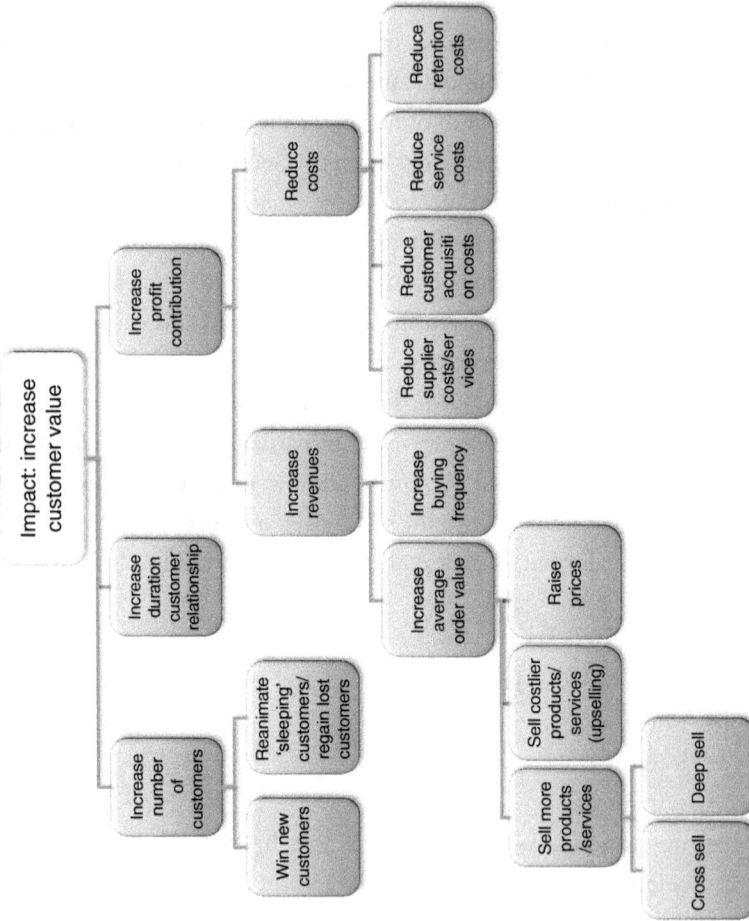

Figure 11.2 The impact on customer value can be seen on many different aspects

the list, one after the other, and get to work on them (once selected, an improvement jumps across to another prioritized list, the *sprint backlog*). The higher an item is on the list, the closer the moment when this will be executed, and so the more detailed the content definition should be. Why this is so, is covered in the following section.

11.2   A New Way of Planning

Within agile management, planning means, more than anything else, prioritizing, and *time-boxing* is a very important aspect of prioritizing. This means that, in practice, meetings and projects always end when the allocated time is up. That forces everyone to separate the wheat from the chaff and get right away to the core tasks. If the duration and frequency of discussions and projects are always the same, it makes planning easier and takes less time. This lets you deal with what really matters: the meaningful work.

Agile management teams work in a fixed iteration rhythm (the "heartbeat"). That is, they always use the same fixed periods to complete their operations from start to finish. The length of this period must be short in order to keep the speed high and to force the teams to make their projects as small as possible. In general, this period is somewhere between one and four weeks, where three weeks is the most-common duration. The period needs to be shorter if the environment is very complex, if there is a lot of dynamics and incidents, if there is much to be adjusted, or if the team is inexperienced. You call this period a *sprint*. *The idea of a sprint* is that the team focuses entirely, during the *sprint*, on the team-chosen activity and nothing else. You are unlikely to ask Usain Bolt for his autograph when he is adjusting his starting blocks for the Olympic 100 meters final.

In a sprint, there is a maximum amount of work the team can do. This capacity is also called the *velocity*. At the beginning of each new iteration, the teams must determine what improvements they *can* and *want* to take on in the coming period. The *can* is then determined by the *velocity*. The *want* has to do with which improvements are at the top of the *product backlog* and how much time these activities will cost. But how do you determine the time needed?

The "Story": What Are You Going to Do for the Customer?

The rough time-estimates you made for the *effort* should therefore be refined, but still not very precise (not, for example like PRINCE2, in which you can graduate via a Gantt chart). That just takes too much time. Above all, plans must be flexible enough to change in response to unforeseen events during their lifetime. To estimate the time required for each improvement, agile management uses a methodology called the *user story*, usually shortened to simply *story*. In a *story*, the team describes, in the simplest possible way, what they want to do and what this will deliver to the customer. As a guideline, you could say that a child or an elderly person should be able to easily understand your *stories*. If you cannot explain it simply, you don't understand it well enough yourself.

Stories are usually structured like this:

as [type of client] I want [to do something] so that I [get a certain benefit]

Here are some examples of stories to follow to give you a better picture:

- As a potential buyer on eBay, I want to see the feedback from other buyers, so that I can judge the quality of the seller.
- As a train traveler, I want to hear directly why the train has stopped and how long it will take to get to my destination, so I can know if I'm going to make my connection.
- As a warehouse worker, I want to be able to directly re-order a product when I see that stock is too low, so I do not always have to walk back to my desk and computer.

The *story* should deliver a so-called *shippable increment,* that means a product or service in a condition fit to be offered to your internal or external client. *If a story* has a larger scope (and therefore cannot be realized in one *sprint*) or multiple *stories* are interdependent, you speak of an *epic.*

The Definition of Done and Working with Points

When the team has "written" the *story*, the following question still must be answered: When do we agree, together, that it is finished, ready? This is what we know as the *Definition of Done.* In order to maintain high quality, it describes when the result is acceptable for the client (the *Product*

Owner). Consider criteria such as: How will a concrete end-result look? Exactly what is it and what isn't it? Has it been tested? Is it already working or still to be implemented? Do we already have customer feedback? Is it documented? And so on.

Finally, it remains to be determined how long it will take to achieve the *story*. Have you ever remodeled your house? Chances are you found out that it was difficult to determine, in advance, the required activities and the time each needed. That's because people are not very good at estimating absolute units of something. But fortunately, we are good at estimating relative stuff: a Great Dane is heavier than a Chihuahua. A useful way to estimate the time needed for a *story*, is to work with a *Points* system, where you are limited to choosing from 1, 2, 3, 5, 8, 13, and 21 points (maybe you recognize the famous Fibonacci sequence). The smallest story gets 1 point and the biggest 21 points. For this to be really useful, it is important that you use this consistently over a long period. In the beginning, it is difficult to assess, and for the team to know, how many *Points* it can handle in one *sprint* (the *velocity*), but one should be confident that the team will discover this for themselves very quickly. Incidentally, if a *story* gets more than 21 *Points*, it should simply be cut up into smaller *stories*, becoming an *epic*.

Meetings

Meetings in agile management should have, as much as possible, the style of a workshop and should be aiming for a specific end-result. Two types of meetings are fundamental to working with agile management, and both should be as short as possible. The first is the *planning meeting, which occurs at the beginning of a new sprint*. As a rule of thumb, you can say a *planning meeting* will take up one hour per week. So in a three-week *sprint*, there will be three hours of *planning meetings*. In advance, the *Product Owner* must ensure that the *stories* on the *product backlog* have been prioritized. During the *Planning Meeting*, and in consultation with the *Product Owner*, the team agrees the *Definition of Done* for the *stories* at the top of the *Product Backlog*. On this basis, the team awards points to these stories. It pulls stories out of the *Product Backlog* and awards them *points,* until the sprint is full. The team then determines the activities required by the *story* and assigns them to the team members. Finally, the team members and the team leader commit to all the agreements they have just made together.

The second type of meeting is the *Daily Standup* (this is also called the *Scrum* and takes its name from the sport of rugby). As the name suggests, this meeting takes place daily at the start of the working day. Moreover, members stand during the meeting, to maintain high energy levels. It may take not more than fifteen minutes. Each team member answers three short questions:

- What have you done since the last *Standup*?
- What are you going to do next?
- Do you need help with something (for example, troubleshooting or removing impediments)?

This way, everyone is quickly informed of the status of each other's work and any issues are resolved quickly. Where necessary, the planning can be adjusted immediately.

Some agile managers use a third type of meeting, called either a *huddle meeting or sync meeting*. This is intended to balance coordination between different teams and so avoid things being done wrong or done twice, or not done. See Figure 11.3 for an overview of these meetings and others we discuss later.

Visualizing the Plan: Working with a Kanban

In Chapter 10, you read that we work visually and in workshop format as much as possible in agile management. This means lots of sketches, cutting and pasting using brown paper, whiteboards, Post-its, and marker pens. Visual working applies to planning also: and here we use a board called a *Kanban*. *It allows the team members to see at a glance the planning and current status. As* Figure 11.4 *shows, on the left is a hierarchical list of all the current sprint stories.* Each *story* will have its own horizontal path, which contains all the activities required for realization of the *story*. These activities change status during the *sprint*. The first status is *To do*. Once execution of an activity begins, it moves one column to the right and gets

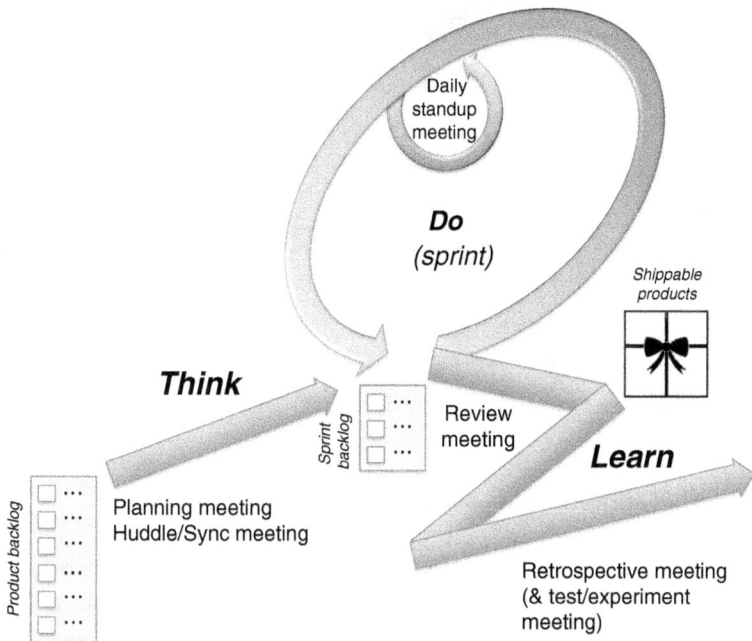

Figure 11.3 The meeting structure around sprints mainly uses Scrum methodologies

the status *Doing*. When the activity is completed, it moves to *Done*. This format can always be refined to meet the specific needs of the team. For example, by breaking-down the *Doing phase* into design, construction, review, and test phases.

Planning discussions always happen with visual support. This ensures the team quickly gets a grip on the schedule. *Planning meetings* and *Daily standups*, therefore, also take place in front of the *Kanban*. And for the *huddle/sync* of *Product Owners* an *effort/impact*-wall and/or a *portfolio*-wall is often used, on which the *Themes* (a cohesive group of ideas aimed at achieving a certain strategic target) and *Epics* are pasted. Thus, it becomes clear where the potential overlaps and blind spots are, and a rough schedule for the medium to long term can be made.

No matter how objective you try to determine the impact and effort of improvements, there will always be a certain degree of subjectivity involved. In order to limit this in the future, as much as possible, it is useful to check what you thought would happen against what actually did happen.

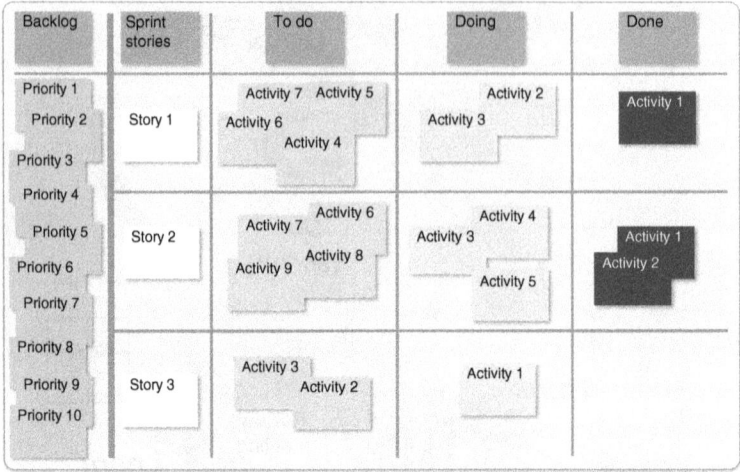

Figure 11.4 A Kanban makes planning visual

So you can learn from what you do and get better at the implementation of the Think phase. Therefore, it is necessary to measure your efforts and results, and this starts with formulating hypotheses. The next section tells you how you go about this.

11.3   Working with Hypotheses and Metrics

Just like the scientific method, agile management works with hypotheses. Obviously, you are not going to invest time and money in an "improvement" unless you expect it to yield a particular result; its *impact*, as discussed in section 11.1. For example, you hope to increase customer satisfaction, or to achieve higher conversion rates. And as Lord Kelvin said: "If you cannot measure it, you cannot improve it."

A hypothesis is a specific statement about your expectations; it makes your assumptions explicit. That statement must be SMART-formulated to make it testable. After the experiment, you should be able to confirm or refute the hypothesis, what we call *verification* and *falsification*. By doing exactly this, you learn from your efforts. You discover what does and does not work; to measure is to know. How do you test a hypothesis? See Chapter 12.

A hypothesis is always formulated as a statement, which may only be proven true or false. Thus, it is black or it is white; it cannot be gray. Some examples:

- Replacing the paper form with a digital form must immediately reduce the duration of the application process by at least 2 days.
- By working with another parts supplier, we save at least $10,000 in the first month.
- Providing a customer with a dedicated contact-person will lead to an increase in customer satisfaction of at least 10 percent within one month.
- By adding said functionality to the site, customer churn will decline by 10 percent within one month.
- The new packaging color will result in a revenue increase of at least 10 percent in the first month.
- A 10 percent price cut will bring at least 1,000 new customers within one month.
- Discontinuing this specific service will not lead to complaints.

As you can see, the hypotheses revolve around certain key performance indicators (KPIs), such as customer satisfaction and customer churn. These KPIs are used to make your hypotheses testable; they form the basis for measurements (also known as *metrics*). When choosing your KPIs, you should think carefully about the distinction between *lagging* and *leading* indicators. Simply put, this means that one is a consequence of the other. Let's clarify this with a simple example: if someone is trying to lose weight, they will regularly stand on their scales to check their weight. This *lagging* indicator is easy to measure, but difficult to influence. What matters is the amount of calories consumed and burned. These *Leading* indicators are exactly the opposite: they are easy to influence, but difficult to measure.

Looking for relevant KPIs? Go to mikehoogveld.com for a list of the 50 most-commonly used KPIs and the associated explanation on how to use these in your hypotheses. When you finish formulating your hypotheses, you have also completed the *Think* phase and are ready to get started with the *Do* phase. Read more about this in Chapter 12.

By reading Chapter 11, you'll have learned the following:
- *Planning is also part of the* Think *phase. Within agile management, planning must proceed quickly and flexibly so that you can focus fully on the content of the* Do *phase. Therefore, you work with time-boxing and a fixed rhythm, as in a* sprint.
- *The first step is to globally-prioritize your inventory of improvement opportunities. You can do that with the* impact/effort-matrix.
- *Next you refine this by translating the improvements into* stories *and assign them* points *for the amount of work each requires. Then you decide which* stories *can be realized in the next* sprint.
- *During the* Planning Meeting, Daily Standups, *and* Huddle/Sync meeting, *planning is discussed visually. You use tools such as* the impact/effort-matrix, Kanban, *and portfolio walls.*
- *To learn from your efforts and their results, it is useful to work with assumptions and KPIs.*

References

1. Parasuraman, A., V. Zeithaml and L. L. Berry. (1988). "SERVQUAL: A Multiple-Item Scale for Measuring Consumer Perceptions of Service Quality." *Journal of Retailing* 64–61, pp. 12–40.
2. Reichheld, F. F. (2003). *The One Number You Need to Grow.* Brighton: *Harvard Business Review.*

CHAPTER 12

Do Phase—Experiment like a Lab Technician

The proof of the pudding is in the eating.
—William Camden

Making your ideas concrete is what this section is all about. You will learn how, through smart design, you can offer your internal or external customer precisely what they need, and how to actually build this design. You discover the usefulness of a *minimum viable product* and how you can test it properly.

12.1 Building Customer-value Propositions

You've put enough thought and planning into the *Think* phase. Now it's time to go to work and prove that your ideas actually work in practice. In other words, prove that your internal or external customer will purchase or use the product or service you create, or value the improvement(s) you make. So you must offer that customer something he appreciates. Whether that is an improved assessment-process in HRM or a new search option in your app, the principle remains the same: how do you offer added value? This concept is called a *customer-value proposition*. Once again, the design and construction of your proposition will benefit from a visual approach, using brown paper, Post-its, and markers. Figure 12.1 shows a format (which comes from the excellent book *Value Proposition Design* by Osterwalder,[1]) which you can put on a whiteboard or brown paper and the one shown is for a vendor-neutral fuel card.

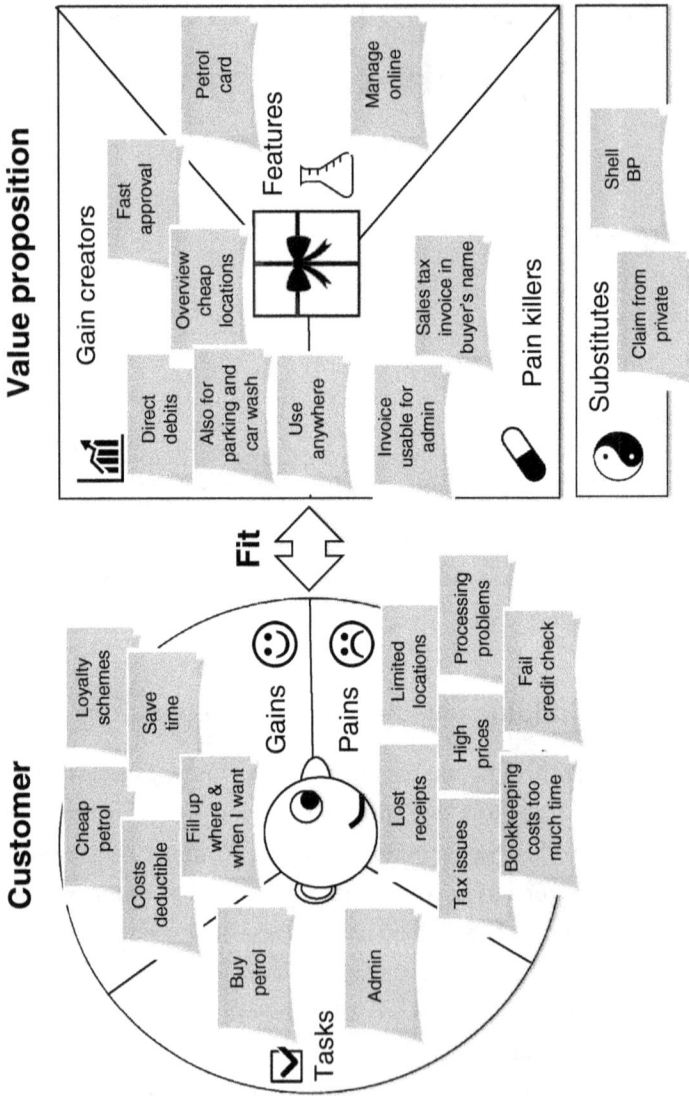

Figure 12.1 The customer value proposition format

Customer-value Proposition

The methodology revolves around the *persona* (see section 10.3). In the example, these are freelancers and other small-business owners. Next, step-by-step, you answer the following questions:

- *What tasks must the customer perform within the framework of what you can and want to offer him? (See also Section 10.3.)*
  This entrepreneur has to fill his vehicle(s) with fuel and keep business accounts for this process.
- *What emotional and rational benefits would the customer thereby gain?*
  He wants to deduct sales taxes and business expenses. Because he is busy, hates bookkeeping, and often makes administrative errors, it must be quick and easy. He also wants to minimize the costs, be able to refuel anywhere and take advantage of loyalty programs.
- *What problems, inconveniences, risks, and barriers might the customer experience?*
  He would fail the credit-check process of the big fuel brands if he applied for their fuel cards. Therefore, he uses his debit card and processes the receipts in his administration. But he often loses receipts and that is not accepted by the tax authorities, so he runs the risk of fines. If he would have a brand-dedicated fuel card, filling-up at another petrol station would just bring similar hassles.
- *What characteristics have your products, services, and channels?*
  A universal fuel card that is coupled to online administration and a supporting app.
- *What is the alternative?*
  A fuel card for the major fuel brands. Or use a private car and claim business mileage.
- *What advantages do your features provide the customer?*
  The pass can be used at all petrol stations. The customer can easily see which are the cheapest garages. Application and approval are possible 24 hours a day online. Direct debit ensures he always

pays immediately. The pass can also be used for parking and the car wash.

- *How do the features solve or ease his pain?*
  Online, automated financial administration ensures his sales tax and costs are always deductible and prevent personal errors. He need not perform time-consuming operations. Furthermore, he is not tied to the sites or the high prices of major fuel brands.

As is apparent from the example, there should be a "fit." The better you can meet the need, the more successful you will be. This is at the core of everything, and you can apply this at any level—to considering a new type of aircraft such as the Dreamliner, developing the first Tesla model, inventing the Netflix service, or expanding payment functionality in a shop. And it gives you a base to optimize continuously. With the fuel card in the example above, you could add functionality with an app that automates the keeping of mileage records, so avoiding additional tax liability. Or a solution for automated-payment when using public transport even only rarely.

A similar development-process is used by Ikea. For over sixty years, Ikea has been a distinctive pioneer in the home furnishings market. Firstly, because the company broke up the traditional market segmentation: buyers of expensive furniture or buyers of cheap furniture. Ikea saw that design need not be expensive, that the combination of cheap and expensive furniture would become a trend and that your life situation affects your choices: whether you are about to study, live together, get children, or buy and furnish a second home. Secondly, Ikea introduced self-service, meaning their furniture was not only cheaper than all their competitors, but could be taken home immediately. Scientific research shows that self-assembling furniture ensures customers better appreciate their purchases.[2]

But, around the turn of the century, Ikea noticed a change. Some customers had no time to assemble their purchases or were not proficient enough and, therefore, found it convenient to have someone assemble it for them. So the company piloted an assembly service which, after some tweaking, was rolled-out across all locations. In addition, Ikea noticed some customers could not transport large items themselves. So Ikea began renting trailers and also offered a delivery service. You'd think they would stop there, but they were constantly looking to improve the customer experience and so increase sales. By walking around the stores, management saw there were also customers who hate shopping, had not enough time for it or simply were not good at finding what they were looking for in the enormous warehouse areas. So Ikea added a service: customers could submit a wish list, which Ikea staff would collect and arrange delivery. And just recently (because Ikea knows how many impulse purchases occur in physical stores) Ikea combined these services into its e-commerce. You can now buy 9,000 Ikea products online, and have them delivered to your door, and have them assembled if you wish. Moreover, Ikea had already, in the late 90s, made headway into the business market with similar solutions.

Back to your *customer-value proposition*. Now the foundations are in place, you need to make sure these manifest in the customer experience. Read more about this in the next section.

12.2 Building Customer Experiences

As the SERVQUAL model makes clear, achieving customer satisfaction is, above all, a matter of matching the expectations of the customer with their perceived experience. In addition to having the right core products and services, it appears that the *customer experience*—at all the organization's touchpoints—also plays a vital role[3]: the customer's actual experience of the proposition, as described in Section 12.1. And that is something your organization can build-on for continuous improvement. But what is a customer experience exactly? Let's look at an example from retail.

Imagine you are in a shoe shop. After a long search, you've finally found the perfect shoes, but the last pair in your size has just been sold. After a deep sigh, you walk over to the cashier and ask if there's a pair in another branch. Like a kind of Sherlock Holmes, the assistant calls one branch after another, searching for the right size. Eventually, you leave the shop, empty-handed, with the vague promise that they will call you. Frustrated, and doubtful if you'll hear from them, you start looking for another shop to begin your search anew. And there goes another chunk of your free time.

At Decathlon, this experience is definitely a thing of the past. In their 1,120 stores worldwide, there are large touch screens with access to their webshop. Here it takes a moment or two to sign up and then you can immediately see the actual stock of all their stores and their central warehouse. You order the product, the machine prints the invoice, and you pay at the checkout. Delivery is free and you get a confirmation mail with your Track & Trace code. Convenient, right? This is useful even when the product is in stock in the store, but you want to continue shopping without having to lug a heavy bag around. Or if you want to see the much larger range in the webshop. Or if you want to receive advice from one of the assistants about products that are never in the shop, such as large fitness equipment. And you can instantly make and purchase personalized products, like a football jersey with your child's name on the back.

With several companies, such as Three (one of the UK's leading mobile operators), it works the other way round: they use an offline channel to improve the online experience. On the site, they meticulously follow your behavior and use these data to predict what you are likely to need. If, for example, you are finding it hard to choose between two subscription packages and clicking from one page to the other, you will get a pop-up screen asking if they can help you directly; for example, by live-chat or phone, after you enter your mobile number. An employee can then guide you to the best choice, by asking you questions and giving expert advice. Customers seem to appreciate this enormously.

Sounds great right? Perhaps you are wondering how Decathlon and Three have so nicely thought through all the issues in detail, and how, perhaps, you could do something similar for your own customers' experiences. For the answer, let's take a trip to the world of film: you are going to use a method called *storyboarding* to describe scenes from the proposed experience. And while you might feel like a third-rate director of a B-movie, you can still put together an awesome script. Everything the customer should experience must be there, obvious, simple, and without nuances. The elements should be clear to everyone in your organization, so they know exactly what is expected of them. Now you can begin thinking through the elements, with your team—a brainstorming session—with brown paper, white boards, Post-its, and marker pens.

Figure 12.2 shows a simplified *storyboard* for an internal customer: a participant in a training course organized by HR. As you can see, the experience is cut up into individual scenes that are described vividly, using colorful imagery. YouTube has a host of funny negative examples we can all relate to; search for "analytics in real life" or "soup nazi."

The elements that emerge in your scenes are the blueprint for creating a concrete customer experience. But you still have to answer the last question, from the business model canvas in Chapter 10, about revenue streams:

- Which features and benefits of our value proposition and channels are our internal/external customers really willing to pay for?
- What are they paying for at the moment? And how do they pay?
- How would they prefer to pay? Consider the following: price per unit of product or service; user fee or licence; subscription; rent/ lease; hourly rates; mediation costs.
- Which pricing mechanism is the best fit, according to the customers? Consider: suggested/list prices; price per quality level or optional product characteristic; volume levels; negotiated price; auctions; real-time market (like shares); yield management (such as airline seats).
- How does each revenue stream add to the total revenue?

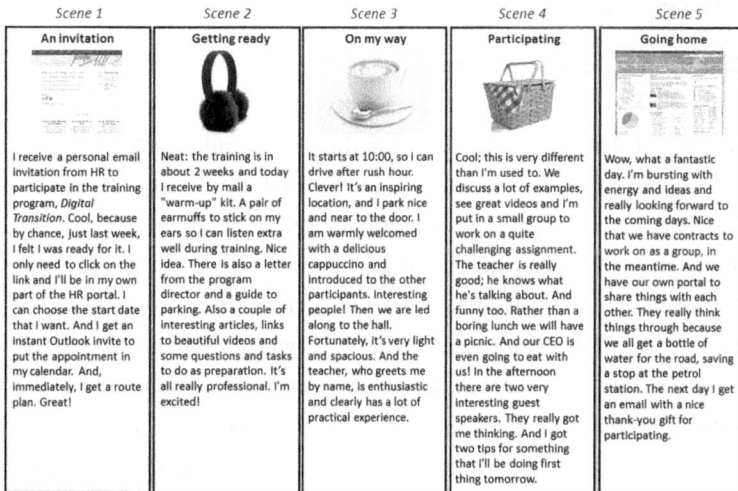

Scene 1	Scene 2	Scene 3	Scene 4	Scene 5
An invitation	**Getting ready**	**On my way**	**Participating**	**Going home**
I receive a personal email invitation from HR to participate in the training program, *Digital Transition*. Cool, because by chance, just last week, I felt I was ready for it. I only need to click on the link and I'll be in my own part of the HR portal. I can choose the start date that I want. And I get an instant Outlook invite to put the appointment in my calendar. And, immediately, I get a route plan. Great!	Neat: the training is in about 2 weeks and today I receive by mail a "warm-up" kit. A pair of earmuffs to stick on my ears so I can listen extra well during training. Nice idea. There is also a letter from the program director and a guide to parking. Also a couple of interesting articles, links to beautiful videos and some questions and tasks to do as preparation. It's all really professional. I'm excited!	It starts at 10:00, so I can drive after rush hour. Clever! It's an inspiring location, and I park nice and near to the door. I am warmly welcomed with a delicious cappuccino and introduced to the other participants. Interesting people! Then we are led along to the hall. Fortunately, it's very light and spacious. And the teacher, who greets me by name, is enthusiastic and clearly has a lot of practical experience.	Cool; this is very different than I'm used to. We discuss a lot of examples, see great videos and I'm put in a small group to work on a quite challenging assignment. The teacher is really good; he knows what he's talking about. And funny too. Rather than a boring lunch we will have a picnic. And our CEO is even going to eat with us! In the afternoon there are two very interesting guest speakers. They really got me thinking. And I got two tips for something that I'll be doing first thing tomorrow.	Wow, what a fantastic day. I'm bursting with energy and ideas and really looking forward to the coming days. Nice that we have contracts to work on as a group, in the meantime. And we have our own portal to share things with each other. They really think things through because we all get a bottle of water for the road, saving a stop at the petrol station. The next day I get an email with a nice thank-you gift for participating.

Figure 12.2 The customer experience of a participant in an in-company training

Now that you've finished your design, it's time to start building. And your tool is the smart approach we met earlier, the *minimum viable product*. How to use it is the theme of the next section.

12.3   Learning Faster and Cheaper with the *Minimum Viable Product*

If you buy a new car, do you buy it immediately or do you take a test drive first? And if it is a used car, do you read the service book or maybe even have the car checked, or do you just assume that it's all right? When you are buying an existing home, do you first visit it and perhaps commission a structural inspection, or do you just buy it directly via a "property portal" such as Zillo and Zoopla? Do you book a hotel or holiday home directly from the site of the travel agent or do you first look for local information and reviews? And what about that interesting new drink that you haven't tried yet? Do you knock it back in one gulp up or start with a careful sip? And the shower or bath? Do you step right in or first put in a hand to feel how hot the water is? Would you immediately marry that (potentially) great partner you met, or do a bit of dating and live together for a while before making such a big decision?

First Try, Then Do

Most people will first perform a kind of test to determine if something comes close to meeting their expectations (SERVQUAL again). It is natural behavior that has been deeply rooted in us for millions of years. We try to eliminate risk by trying something out carefully and if it proves to be safe, we continue. Just as animals do: first sniff a bit and then take a bite. An instinct that helps you survive.

The strange thing is that in organizations, it often works differently. There are countless examples of investments where a lot of money was put in, only to find, long after at the launch, that the product is not working properly or that customers do not need it. As you read earlier, this way of proceeding is called the "waterfall" approach. This occurs internally, such as in IT projects in government institutions, but also externally. The latter is most evident in products and services for consumers. Take for example the market introductions New Coke, the BMW C1 scooter, Persil Power, and computer-voting. There is even a museum of failed products. Annually, an estimated 156,000 new products come to market, a new-product launch on average every three minutes. And 76 percent fail.[4]

This return may be higher, but for that we need to transcend alchemy. That organizations innovate is, of course, very nice. But when intelligence and structure are brought into the experiment, the results can be improved—with a predictability which would make a *match fixer* very happy.

Reviewing Your Production

Agile management takes a logical approach to improving results. In Chapter 11, you read all about the *story* and the *definition of done*. These serve to deliver, at the end of a *sprint*, an improvement that works and has been tested "technically." To determine whether it does do what it is supposed to do, the team performs an inspection with the product owner and any other interested parties. This informal meeting is called a *review* and lasts not more than two hours. The aim is to promote cooperation by looking together at what has been accomplished during the *sprint*. On the basis of their feedback and the ideas generated during this meeting, the value of what has just been made can be further increased, and the *product-backlog* immediately adjusted.

Another important success factor in the approach is the *minimum viable product* (MVP). Let's look at what that means.

MVP: Back to Basics

The *MVP* (serial-entrepreneur Steve Blank calls it the *minimum feature set*) is a concept which allows you, with the minimum possible cost and at the highest possible speed, to learn how much your internal or external customers appreciate your products, services, and experiences or the improvements you've made to these. The simpler the better (like the story in section 11.2). Instead of spending a lot of time and money trying to create a perfect, ready-to-use product, you strip away everything, except what is absolutely necessary, until you're left with something that is just about viable. So you can get faster feedback from your customers and avoid unnecessarily investing in tasks to which the customer attaches no value (the *Lean value-creation* which you read about in paragraph 7.3). So you first try-out what you've made before you improve it further, so as to avoid wastage. In other words, you can smart-test the hypotheses that you generated in the *Think* phase. That is the purpose of the *MVP* and fits perfectly with the rapid iterations of the *Think–Do–Learn* cycle.

The limits to the viability of an *MVP* are determined by the customer: which quality level is acceptable to him, in terms of completeness and predictability of performance? Conversely, you want to learn as quickly as possible, plus you want to work as cheaply as possible in terms of the amount of time and money you invest. These three factors give you a dilemma, as you can never score well on all three criteria. You have to be smart here and look for the best balance (see Figure 12.3).

How does this work exactly? Architects, for example, work with 3D software and models to talk through their designs with a client. Film studios show animated storyboards, and sometimes rough trailers to panels of frequent moviegoers. Car makers create mock-ups of studio models and show these *concept cars* at trade shows to gather reactions

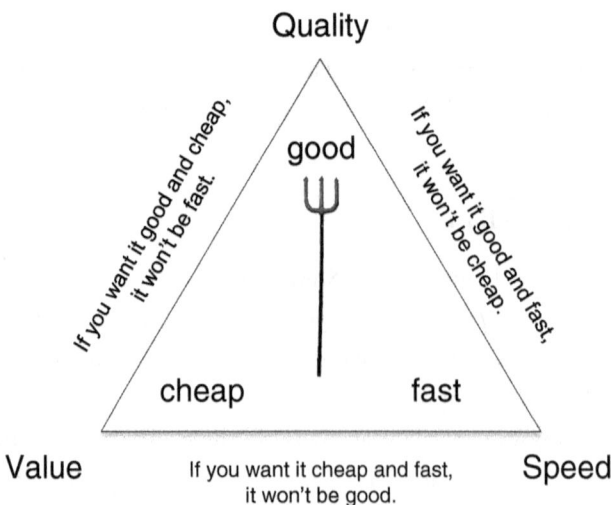

Figure 12.3 The devilish dilemma of the minimum viable product

from media and potential customers. Comedians first do tryouts in small venues before they go into a real theater. Fashion designers create sketches of their clothes and match them with fabric samples to demonstrate their new designs to the decision makers at the big brands.

The idea is that, via the *MVP*, your customers get a good understanding of what you want to offer them eventually, an unusual application of *fake it until you make it*. This seems to work best with *early adopters*, a term coined by Everett Rogers.[5] Early adopters are lovers of innovation, they like to try new things, and so are open to an *MVP*. They are visionary enough to imagine the missing features themselves, if necessary. Another advantage is that you can also use *early adopters* to engender enough curiosity in the *early majority* to make them want to try your proposition out. This effect is called *crossing the chasm*[6]: bridging the critical gap to the practically minded and more-expectant masses.

What shape can your *MVP* take? Here is a nonexhaustive list of commonly used forms suitable for internal and external customers:

- *Idea or concept*—If you have an idea or concept in your head or have put one on paper, for example using the right-hand section of the *business model canvas*, you can investigate this with your (potential) customers in *key interviews* and *focus groups* (you could go even further by running co-creation sessions.) Or you can discuss the idea or concept via your own blog page, so you can gauge the reactions of visitors and get into discussions with them.
- *Mock-up*—Here you take the next step and let your (potential) customers see your concept: it might be a clay model, a mood board, or a wireframe that you show them. Or a *landing page* on which you show fake product images or screenshots. When visitors click through for more information or to order, they get an error message, or a message that it is temporarily sold-out or otherwise unavailable. Or they come to a page where they can sign up for a (free) trial, or can subscribe to get an email as soon as it is available, or even order the product in advance. You attract visitors to the landing page by promoting it on your website, or via a Google adwords campaign, or a (viral) campaign using social media.

- *Demo*—Going one step further, you can offer a demonstration of your service/product, by putting an explanatory video on the landing page (this is how Dropbox started), or create a fake site where you click through and make it appear to really work.
- *Prototype*—The next step is a working beta-version of the proposition, a one-off makeshift product a bit like a patchwork quilt: a bit from here; a bit from there. To do this, there are all kinds of cloud solutions available: platforms like Amazon Web Services and Google Forms. Sometimes, you have to do some manual work behind the scenes, which will ultimately be automated. You can choose to imply that it is all automated or you can be fully transparent to your users. Zappos.com, for example, started with the first approach. Finally, you can also choose not to display "all" your features in limited form, but only one more or fully developed feature, the most important of course. And here Google is the killer example.

The *MVPs* discussed above show that it often involves a combination of the form of the product and the test method. However, some test methods are suitable for multiple forms and some forms are suitable for multiple testing methods. Therefore, it is good to look at the test methods separately. This we do in Section 12.4.

12.4   Testing: to Measure Is to Know

Imagine that you are working for a sports brand, which has been producing sports footwear for more than forty years. You notice a retro trend in the market and wonder if there might be demand for a vintage model. But you know that it would be far too expensive to just take the gamble and produce a series. That old chicken-and-egg problem. How can you solve this? By going to your product archives, selecting some old models, photographing them, and putting them on eBay. If enough people look at them and place bids for them, you will get a good indication of the potential. If it is large enough, you decide which models to get back into production. That is the way Nike did it.

Another useful insight can be when you realize that there are people who believe enough in your product or service that they are willing to invest in it. And these are not professional investors, but people who could also be your clients; crowdfunding. There are numerous platforms where you can organize crowdfunding easily and quickly, such as Kickstarter; if it works, it also increases your working capital.

What the above makes clear is that within agile management, there are actually two types of tests. As Section 11.3 showed already, you first do a *technical* test on what you have built. The aim is to determine whether what you've built works. In addition, as the Nike and crowdfunding examples above demonstrate, you also want to test its *customer potential.* This type of testing we discuss below.

Commitments rather than Words

So what you do, in this type of test, is look at how customers and prospects respond to what you have designed for them, whether it is a tangible product, an online service, or an improvement in the functioning of a specific channel. And as much as you might do some exploring in the initial phase, by asking customers about their needs and preferences, you really want to know if they will, eventually, actually go out and buy or use what you are offering them.

You immediately come up against a problem which, in 1962, David Ogilvy identified: "People do not *think* what they *feel*, do not *say* what they *think* and do not *do* what they *say.*" Since then, this has been confirmed by neurological research. Scientists might argue about the exact percentage, but 90 to 95 percent of our behavior seems to be unconscious. Functional MRI (fMRI) scans provide hard evidence of this phenomenon: our brain has made a decision for us on average seven seconds before "we" think we make that decision.[6] These unconscious decisions, in practice, appear very reliable, so researchers use them as a basis for predictions. When an fMRI of people seeing, for example, three different *Cosmopolitan* covers, shows that one version generates the most buying impulses, it also later appears, by far to do best in newsstand sales. Yet the research subjects themselves cannot say exactly why they chose that particular cover.

For example, you want to buy a house and you are going to look at some houses. As soon as you put your foot on the garden path, your brain has already decided if it is going to be this house or not. But you still sit down afterwards and try to make a rational decision, for example by drawing up a list of pros and cons, which you might even weigh and score. Very objective, right? Not so. Your brain continues, unconsciously, to control the selection, weighting and scoring your arguments so that your results seamlessly match what it has already decided for you. Your brain makes everything fit in with what has already been established, in order to prevent *cognitive dissonance*. However, we think of ourselves as rational beings and classic market research is based on this idea. You talk to customers, using surveys, focus groups, and interviews, mostly asking about intentions for future behavior in hypothetical situations. But the effect of unconscious behavior calls into question the predictive value of this approach.

What is the best way to test if the results do have a high predictive value? Not with words but with deeds: you shouldn't talk to your customers, but observe their actual behavior, and not like an old-fashioned spy behind a newspaper with two eyeholes cut into it. Fortunately, there are much better sources of information, as you will see in Chapter 13. But in the next paragraph, you can already find out more about the most important source.

The AB(C) Test

For many organizations, it is a challenge to test in a pure and objective way. The first and major obstacle is what they call, at Google, the "HiPPO" effect (*Highest Paid Person's Opinion*): teams allow their decision-making to be influenced, too much, by the opinions of their leaders. And therein are great risks. It is vital that your conclusions are as factual as possible (see Figure 12.4). On the podium of analysis, facts get the gold medal, while arguments, experiences, and *guesstimates* get silver. And in third place are assertions and opinions, which you would be better off disqualifying and taking the bronze away. As Deming said: "In God we trust, all others bring data."

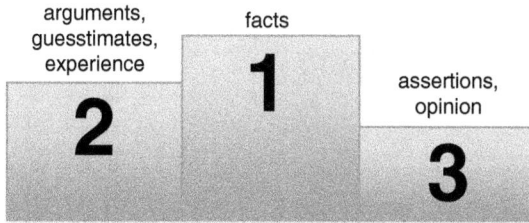

Figure 12.4 Focus in testing as much as possible on hard factual data

So think of yourself as a chemist in a laboratory, and work as objectively and as structured as possible. Precision is essential. Your hypotheses from the *Think* phase, which you obviously did not formulate for nothing, should now serve as the basis for what you are going to test. And an important principle comes into play: *ceteris paribus*—and that's not one of Harry Potter's magical spells. The literal meaning of this Latin phrase is: *with other conditions remaining the same*. In other words, we try to change just one thing at a time, so that we can measure its impact, isolated from and excluding everything else. Difficult? It turns out to be easier than you think.

This is really well suited to an A/B-test, aka a *split-run* test (see Figure 12.5). Suppose you want to change the packaging of a product to increase sales volume. So, of course, you want to find out what adjustments work or not. In half of the selection of representative stores, you place the new packaging, of which one aspect has been changed, for example, the background color. In the other half of the stores, you leave the existing packaging. If the new packaging appears to attract higher sales than the old, you know the background color is a success factor. And that is possible because you can make a comparison with what is called the "control group." This approach can be applied anywhere. To the format of a call-center script, a font in your application, the place of a button in your webshop, the order of an online form, traffic routing in your store, and so on. You can also expand the number of variants, for example to three, and that's your ABC test.

Now that you've built and tested your adjustments, it is time to evaluate the results. You want to know whether the implementation of your plans and the ensuing results match your hypotheses. You can read more about this in Chapter 13, which deals with the *Learn* phase.

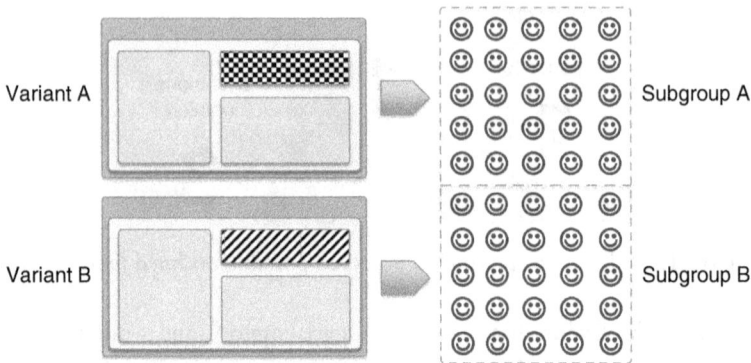

Figure 12.5 *The principle of the A B testing*

By reading this chapter, you'll have discovered the following:

- *You can make your ideas for changes and improvements concrete, by working them into a* customer-value *proposition. In it you translate the benefits sought by your internal and external customers, and the problems they experience in performing their customer jobs, into a suitable solution.*
- *In order to design and build the ideal customer experience of this solution, you can employ the storyboard approach.*
- *To find out quickly and cheaply if your solution is relevant and functioning properly, you can use a* minimum viable product *(MVP). This can take the form of an idea, concept, mock-up, demo, or prototype. The MVP is actually a form and test method combined.*
- *The testing is done on the basis of the hypotheses from the* Think *phase. With your choice of test methodology, it is important above all to observe the actual behavior of your internal or external customers, and to ensure you perform your measurements in a* ceteris paribus *situation. An A/B test fits perfectly here.*

References

1. Osterwalder, A., and Y. Pigneur. (2014). *Value Proposition Design.* Hoboken: Wiley.
2. Norton, D., and D. M. Ariely. (2012). The IKEA Effect: When Labor Leads to Love. *Journal of Consumer Psychology* 22–23, pp. 453–460.

3. Service 2020: Return on service. (2014). Economist Intelligence Group.
4. Lindstrom, M. (2009). *Buyology*. New York: Random House Business.
5. Rogers, E. (2013). *Diffusion of Innovations*. New York: Free Press.
6. Moore, G., and R. McKenna. (2009). *Crossing the Chasm*. New York: HarperCollins.

CHAPTER 13

The Learn Phase—Stepping Smarter into the Future

Having heard it is not as good as having seen it;
having seen it is not as good as knowing it;
knowing it is not as good as putting it into practice.

—Xunzi (312–230 BC)

You've arrived at the final step of the agile process: the *Learn* phase. Based on your plans and how their implementation went, you want to find out what worked well and what did not. How to tackle this is the theme of this chapter. It covers the resources available to you and how you can use them for your evaluation. And what to do when your evaluation is complete.

13.1   Evolving through Evaluation

The final step in the *Think–Do–Learn* process is dominated by analysis. Structured evaluation of your efforts and results enables you to learn from the past what you should do in the future. It's here that continuous improvement is made very concrete.

Self-Evaluation: The "Retrospective"

The evaluation process was already partly setup during the *review* meeting of the *Do* phase, covered in Section 12.3. That *review* brings insights that are then placed on the *product backlog*. In addition, there is still another meeting, the two-hour-maximum *retrospective*. It is here, at the end of a *sprint,* that the team looks critically at their own approach; among other outcomes, it ensures the team avoids making the same mistakes again in the next iteration. This *retrospective,* therefore, takes place at a meta-level and has one simple aim, to get better. You can compare it to the cars of a roller coaster being hoisted up to the start of the ride. The process is accompanied by a loud clicking sound coming from the fuse (and possibly the more-nervous passengers). This fuse ensures that the trolleys cannot fall-back, out-of-control, should the power fail. That's what you want to achieve with the *retrospective*: always moving at least one step further up, with the certainty that you will not drop back (and the fervent hope that you will not feel sick from the roller-coaster ride).

The *retrospective* can work quickly and visually, for example by sticking Post-its—that address a particular criterion—onto brown paper. Example issues might include job satisfaction, team atmosphere, quantity and quality of what is produced, conduct of meetings (*standup* planning; *review*), workload, *story* points, workflow, collaboration, flexibility of output, and so on. Next to each criterion, you draw a line with a scale of 1 to 10. Each team member can then put their own stickers on the line of their choice. Then, for each criterion, a global average is calculated so that it soon becomes clear what are the opportunities for improvement. This list is a useful starting point for a debate. However, it is key here, again and again, to ask the *why* question in a constructive way, in order to discover what we call the *root cause*. The discussion should lead to SMART formulated actions, preferably documented for the purpose of knowledge sharing.

Evaluating the Test Results

In addition to this self-evaluation, the team should also look at the effect the improvements they delivered have had on their internal or external customers. For this latter step, you return to your hypotheses from the *Think* phase, to determine whether, on the basis of your metrics, they have been confirmed or rejected. At the *story* level, look at the measurements that emerged from your tests. What do you see happening in the customer behavior? Has what you have offered the customer been used and appreciated? Does this realize your goals? You look, in other words, at to what extent the test results meet your expectations and whether the implementation went as planned. The next question: Is the latest adjustment or outcome now the new standard? If so, what is there further to improve? If not, do you need to look for an alternative?

The form in which this evaluation takes place varies greatly between and within organizations. Sometimes, there is only a small improvement or a short test period, for which a quick discussion is enough. Teams often hold a formal meeting (often called a *test meeting* or *experiment meeting*), in which multiple tests are evaluated. Obviously, meetings should be planned to fit in with the *sprint*-rhythm, to avoid *sprint* activities or tests becoming redundant. In *Lean* terminology, this would be seen as waste.

As we saw in Section 12.4, you need to design and evaluate your testing process to ensure you proceed as objectively as possible. The search, for relationships between effort and results is, in fact, an art in itself. Unfortunately, most people practice *jumping to conclusions* at an Olympic level. They sometimes confuse correlation with causality: there is a connection, but no cause–effect relationship. Or they turn this relationship around, basically arguing that the sun rises because the rooster crows. Sometimes they fit other fallacies around their "beliefs," such as errors in logic, false assumptions, incorrect semantics, no burden of proof, circular reasoning, and so on. Therefore, someone in the meeting must take the role of critically questioning the reasoning and factual evidence. This role is most often called the *challenger* (comparable to De Bono's *white hat*).

Naturally, visualization is again very valuable when evaluating your tests. As the English say "A picture paints a thousand words": graphics are faster, easier, and thus, better understood than complex sets of figures and texts. Resources such as an Ishikawa diagram, decision tree, box plot, histogram, and cross-table can help you. Furthermore, you should be careful when working with averages because, sometimes, they can be misleading or even impossible (how many parents do you know with 1.6 kids?), even if you only use them for identifying trends in a time-series. A particularly easy pitfall is to look at the overall figures for the whole group, when what you need to do is look at the separate subgroups within. An example: since the launch of your new app a year ago, you can see that the cumulative number of downloads, registrations, logins, and active users is still rising rapidly. A hockey-stick curve; must be good news. Right? Closer examination reveals it is not. If you look at the number of "cohorts"[1] per month, you see that, in recent months, the number of downloads has continued to climb, but the percentage of downloaders who then go on to register is actually going down. And of those who do register, fewer and fewer login again. So all the improvements you realized are not bringing you an increased return from any of the new groups. In *Lean* terms, this means that you are wasting time, effort, and money: your investment in increasing the number of downloads, does not add enough value because you are decreasing the conversion rate.

In short, the better you're able to look at the behavior of your internal and external customers, the more quickly and effectively you can customize the next improvement cycle. The following section shows you what information sources are available to you.

13.2   Sources: The "Voice of the Customer"

Do you remember those childhood puzzles where you had to connect numbered dots with a pencil line? It was only at the end, when you had connected all the dots, that you saw the whole picture. Only then did you understand what you had drawn. It works in pretty much the same way when you're analyzing your internal or external customers. By combining information from different sources, you can get a complete picture of the needs and behaviors of your customer. Within Lean, this is known as the *voice of the customer* (VOC). The idea behind the VOC is that the customer is always taken as the starting point for improvement, as you saw in Chapter 10: the persona and customer journey. First, listen to the customer. Because, as Epictetus said: "Nature has given men one tongue but two ears, so we can listen twice as much as we speak."

The VOC, in agile management, has a kind of dual role, in that it serves two purposes. When for the first time, you work through the *Think–Do–Learn* cycle, during the *Think* phase, you use the VOC to analyze your internal or external customers and to capture this analysis in a *persona* and *customer journey*. Then you can use the VOC information for your measurements and testing, which you learned how to do in Chapter 12. The insights provided by this, of course, in turn, become the basis for the *Think* phase in the next iteration. With the VOC, therefore, you look both backwards and forwards, and thus, it represents a fulcrum in the *Think–Do–Learn* cycle.

Section 12.4 also showed that not all VOC sources are suitable for all purposes. The strength of the approach lies mostly in combining different types of information. This is known as *triangulation*. Compare it with the triangulation of GPS satellites to determine the exact position of your car. But what sources of information are there? Figure 13.1 gives an overview.

Figure 13.1 shows a distinction between passive and active sources. With passive sources, your internal or external client is unaware that he is being studied. He is not affected by the investigation, so you can safely assume that this is a "pure" situation that he is behaving normally. With active sources, this is not the case, and you have to look critically at the potential impact of the research itself on the customer's behavior. Throughout there is a distinction between qualitative and quantitative information. With qualitative information, you should take care to ensure that the results are statistically reliable and suitable to be projected onto the entire population.

Each of the quadrants has its own specific added value. So, for example, actively obtained qualitative information in particular, is suitable for

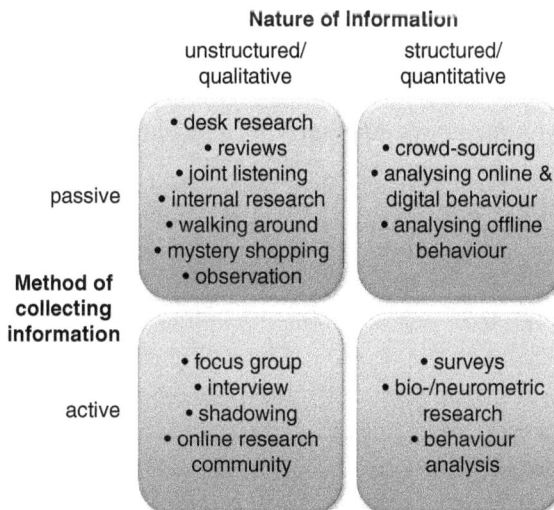

Nature of Information

	unstructured/ qualitative	structured/ quantitative
passive	• desk research • reviews • joint listening • internal research • walking around • mystery shopping • observation	• crowd-sourcing • analysing online & digital behaviour • analysing offline behaviour
active	• focus group • interview • shadowing • online research community	• surveys • bio-/neurometric research • behaviour analysis

Method of collecting information

Figure 13.1 The various types of sources within the VOC[2]

explorative research, in which you find *eye openers* and discover the key narratives of certain topics. Passively obtained quantitative information is very suitable for experiments such as A/B testing. But, as I said, the strength is in the combination of the different approaches and their sources.

Incidentally, it is always a combination of *science & art*, as there is always the need for a healthy dose of intuitive entrepreneurship. As sociologist William Bruce Cameron said, *"Not Everything that can be counted counts, and not everything can be counted that counts."* And Einstein stated about this: *"Logic will get you from A to B. Imagination will take you everywhere."* Steve Jobs also expressed this beautifully in his biography[3]:

> Some people say 'Give the customers what they want'. But that's notmy approach. Our job is to figure out what they're going to want beforethey do. I think Henry Ford once said, 'If I'd asked customers what theywanted, they would have said a faster horse!' People don't know whatthey want until you show it to them. That's why I never rely on marketresearch. Our task is to read things that are not yet on the page.

It always begins with curiosity, whether you run the analysis yourself or bring in data-mining specialists. The sources agile management uses are discussed in more detail below.

Resources for an Active Approach to Acquiring Qualitative Information

The most relevant sources here are:

- *Focus group* (also called a *customer panel)*—In these flexible group interviews, you can ask a lot of in-depth questions. So they are well suited to issues such as needs, motivations, criteria, preferences, orientation, and purchasing behavior.
- *Individual depth-interview*—The main difference between this and a focus group is that the individual is not affected by other participants, either negatively (*group pressure*) or positively (*new*

angles and ideas). On the one hand, this means that his answers come closer to his real personal "truth"; on the other hand, it requires more creativity and skill, from the interviewer, to ask questions that are broad in range and address different angles. Moreover, you can also use customer panels and interviews to allow respondents to get acquainted with your products and services while you observe this process, possibly in combination with asking questions about your observations.

- *Customer shadowing*—A day "following" in the customer's footsteps gives practical insights into their behavior in relation to your products and services, but has the great, unavoidable, disadvantage that your presence creates *bias*.
- *Online research community*—In a protected online environment, a moderator periodically invites panelists, by e-mail, to answer questions about the use of certain products and services, or to give their views on specific topics. As this concerns long-running research, it can also measure trends.

Resources for an Active Approach to Acquiring Quantitative Information

The most relevant sources here are:

- *Surveys*—surveys are usually completed online (and differ from an online research community in that a *survey* only happens once) following an e-mail invitation or a pop-up on a website. In addition, many are still contacted by telephone, both *outbound* and *inbound* (such as after a complaint call to customer service). Finally, there is also significant face-to-face work done in the field, for instance by questioning visitors to an exhibition or shop and gathering the data with the aid of a tablet.
- *Bio-/neurometric research*—This would include fMRI and EEG brain scans and *eyetracking*. All three methods involve the subjects being exposed to concrete things, such as a website or product, in order to determine which areas of their brains show activity as they react emotionally, and where their attention focuses.

- *Behavioral analysis*—These include viewing, listening, and surfing habits for television, radio, desktops, tablets, and smartphones, measured using set-top boxes or software.

Sources for a Passive Approach to Acquiring Qualitative Information

The most relevant sources here are:

- *Desk research*—Reports, reviews, trend analyses, literature etc. based on completed research around issues like trends, market developments, brand perception, needs, and competition.
- *Reading reviews, test reports, and news or opinion articles*—These can come from consumer associations, consumers on *special interest* sites, or journalists. This gives an indication of the criteria against which your products and services are being assessed and how your organization scores against those criteria, possibly in comparison with competitors.
- *Listen in on call center/face-to-face conversations*—You can also read the call-center logs or study call reports. This allows you to determine what support customers need, what questions or complaints they have, and what information they request.
- *Internal research*—Reading emails, app and text messages, tweets, and completed complaint forms make clear what are the more-extreme experiences, positive and negative, and on what these experiences are based. Exchanged or returned products and warranty claims make product defects clear and demonstrate how customers experienced products in use: what they look for, what they find important, what requirements the product must meet, and what is expected of the exchange/return process. You will gain insight into which products are exchanged or returned most often and, sometimes, why that happens.
- *Walking around*—If you personally, "undercover," replace a shop-assistant or call-center employee or *field sales executive*, you will benefit from being in direct contact with the customer. This also provides practical insights into what can be improved in the customer experience, but from the perspective of the one providing this experience.

- *Mystery shopping*—Here you "get under the skin" of your internal or external customers. Again, you'll get practical insights into what is going well in the customer experience offered within your channels, and what needs to be improved.
- *Observations*—These can be spontaneous observations in the form of anecdotes, personal experiences, and culture clues. This can be more targeted by using, for example, a customer "safari" in shopping centers or at trade fairs and events. This could also take place in your own or competitor's stores. This provides general input about what customers do, how they behave, and other valuable data.

Sources for a Passive Approach to Acquiring Quantitative Data

The most relevant sources here are:

- *Crowdsourcing*—By actively engaging your customers in initiatives you develop and promote, you can learn a lot. Earlier, you read about the potential in crowdfunding, but you can also learn and bond with your customers through *co-creation*. You can organize this both offline and online. Nike does this online with *NIKEiD*, where customers can design their own shoes. The choices they make while doing so provide Nike with superb data about their current and future preferences, upon which it bases its future product range and designs. LEGO does something similar, letting customers design their own kits and bring in their own ideas. The latter initiative led to LEGO's most successful product ever: *LEGO Friends*.
- *Behavior on your organization's website and apps*—Within your own site and app is obviously the place to gather a wealth of information: landing pages, logins, click paths and patterns, reactions, *calls to action*, downloads, orders, filling-in forms, live chats, device type (PC, tablet, smartphone), and so on. By analyzing these data, you can learn a tremendous amount about your customers. It lends itself very well to, for example, A/B tests.
- *Social-media behavior*—By tracking relevant topics on social media like Facebook, Twitter, and LinkedIn, you can quickly learn what the opinion or attitude is of customers toward e.g. your brand,

organization, products, services, campaigns, promotions, service, and your competitors.

- *Other online behavior*—Analyzing data such as the terms used in search-engine fields, home pages, *click throughs* on ads, and *retargeting responses,* can provide you with useful insights. You can also measure very specifically between online (and offline) channels using QR codes, source codes and unique URLs, phone numbers, and freepost addresses.

- *Other digital and offline behavior*—Systems usage can also provide important insights. For internal customers you can study intranet use, HRM administration, and other applications. For external customers, this can involve such things as digital kiosks, cash-register records, scans, debit and loyalty card use, and e-mail. You can measure the number of visitors in your stores ("footfall") through electronic counters or cameras at the entrances. If customers use the WiFi your shops provide, via three-point measurements, you can create a *heat map* of their movement around the shop floor. And, of course, it is quite easy to capture their contact with the call center or field sales.

In short, no lack of potential sources. The challenge is to use them, and the information they provide, as objectively as possible. For, as Anaïs Nin said, "We do not see things as they are, we see things as we are." The findings mean that you can adjust quickly. But how do you determine whether you need to adjust? Read below.

13.3   It's Your Choice: Continue or Pivot

Section 13.1 talked about the *test/experiment* meeting, which focuses on evaluating your results. Based on the measurements you've made with help from the VOC sources, you determine how much you can confirm or reject your hypotheses. Depending on the outcome, there are three decisions you can make. With the first two, you continue with what you were doing but, with the last, you change course quite sharply:

- *New default*—If results have indeed improved, use your approach now as your new standard, your *baseline*. In the next iteration, you get started with refining this baseline with either additional improvements or entirely different improvements.

- *Looking for alternatives*—When there's no or insufficient improvement, you go into the next iteration looking for other solutions that do produce the desired result.
- *Pivoting*—Sometimes you make an accidental discovery, as discussed in Section 4.4 that turns your vision or ideas upside down. Or you conclude that your approach has yielded insufficient or no improvement—or maybe even a deterioration, while there are no obvious alternatives. At that point, you have to make a more fundamental choice, which we call a *Pivot*.

Pivoting

Pivot, within the context of agile management, means "turning point." If you are at a dead end, you go back to your last crossing, and take a new road, set a new course. That crossing is represented by those elements in your approach that have actually proven themselves, the elements which you are sure are successful. If you compare it with mountaineering, you can see it as your *basecamp*. Once you determine that the route you are taking, to establish a new camp at a higher altitude, will not succeed, you can always return to your *basecamp* and try a new approach or another route the next day.

Within agile management, there are multiple *pivot* points, for both your internal and your external customers. These *pivot* points are related to the components of the *business model canvas*, which you read in section 10.1. The most important are shown below:

- *Target group*—Sometimes, you find out that a different market segment makes use of your products or services than you originally imagined. You can then leave your proposition unchanged, but you will need to focus on a different audience. For example, this happened with the Peugeot 1007, which was originally intended as a trendy city car but, because of its convenient sliding doors, was mainly purchased by the elderly.
- *Proposition*—It may turn out that a product or service meets a need for your customers, but is less important than you expected. Or

it meets a customer's need in a way that you never unexpected: walkie-talkies and home telephone sets for example were used as baby monitors; the same happened when mobile telephony subscriptions started offering unlimited calls. Then you keep your target group, but you need to reposition or renew your product or service; for example, by making one of the characteristics of your product, service, or experience the most important, or even to ignore all the other characteristics. The converse is also possible: you just add components to the previously single part. This is called *zooming-in* and *zooming-out*. This is exactly what Amazon did when it broadened its offerings from only books and CDs to include electronics, toys, and so on.

- *Channel*—Section 10.4, about *customer journeys*, already discussed that consumers use *channels* when finding, buying, and using your products and services. Sometimes, they seem to prefer other channels than you expected. Or channel conflicts arise with your partners. Then you can choose to use your channels differently, or to use different channels. Long before the Internet age, the computer manufacturer Dell had already decided to deliver directly to the end customer, thus eliminating the middlemen.

- *Income streams*—As an organization, you might learn that your products and services do not realize the revenue streams that you had planned for. Then you need to adjust your business model. Ebay subsidiary *Marktplaats,* for example, did this as soon as it became clear that their model of "free ads but pay for additional services" was making a loss. *Marktplaats* then decided to ask €6 for advertisements for products with a value greater than €200 and also for services. And later, this was adapted into differentiated tariffs for different product-areas and advertisement duration.

- *Cost*—The profitability of your business can sometimes be hindered by certain activities generating excessive costs. Then you can choose to in- or outsource them, or to switch to a technology that offers a better price–performance ratio. Sometimes, it even has an impact on your channels and revenue streams, such as at Netflix. Netflix originally rented-out DVDs, which they mailed to the customer. With the advent of broadband Internet connections, they switched to a streaming model, which had much lower costs, allowing them to change their business model.

- *Platform*—Sometimes, companies find that the way they offer their products and services can also be used by third parties. They approach them and offer a platform: Amazon now allows third parties to sell through its webshop, and offers its proprietary technology as a cloud service called Amazon Web Services.

Through your *evaluations,* you have either a) chosen the approach that will be your new standard, b) to seek out alternatives, or c) to *pivot.* This brings you to the end of the *Think–Do–Learn* cycle. So it's time, based on what you've learned, to start a new iteration. And when that iteration is complete, you start a new one, again and again. So, ad infinitum they follow each other until the cycle becomes second nature.

But what if you still need to start your **very first** iteration? If your organization has yet to make the transition to agile management? In the next and final chapter, you can read about the do's and don'ts of implementing agile management.

By reading this chapter, you'll have discovered the following:
- *In the Learn phase, analysis is central. This is done on two levels: first, look during the* retrospective *meta-level meeting at your own activities, to evaluate whether you can improve your approach. Second, look at the test results to determine if your hypotheses are confirmed or rejected. Preferably, this would also be done during the* retrospective, *but it can also be in a separate meeting, which is usually referred to as the* test *or* experiment *meeting.*
- *The VOC gives you information for both analyzing your customers and making measurements during your testing. Thus, this is a turning point in the* Think–Do–Learn *cycle.*
- *Within the VOC, distinction is made between* passive *and* active *sources and also* quantitative *and* qualitative *information. The four groups which arise as a result offer their own specific values, wherein the power is in the combination of the different types.*
- *Based on the confirmation or rejection of your assumptions, you can take one of three decisions: choose your approach with your new*

standard, find alternatives, or pivot. *The latter means that your approach changes, fundamentally. That can be along the lines of target groups, propositions, channels, revenue streams, costs, and platforms.*

References

1. Ries, E. (2011). *The Lean Startup*. New York: Crown Publishing
2. Thanks to Robert Ossenbruggen.
3. Isaacson, W. (2011). *Steve Jobs*. London: Simon & Schuster.

CHAPTER 14

Becoming Future-Proof

If there is no struggle, there is no progress.
—Frederick Douglass

You should now have both a theoretical and a practical understanding of agile management. And perhaps you are feeling so positive about it that you are considering implementing it in your own organization. How do you do that? How do you ensure that your organization is *built to last*? And what should you be looking out for? That's the story of this final chapter.

14.1 Agile Managing: Back to the Core

You may think, however, as you come to the end of this book, that it is all rather obvious. Great! Because the best thing that can happen is that this book, very quickly, makes itself redundant. In essence, agile management is pure logic and is not *rocket science*. It goes back to the basics of entrepreneurship.

But, in this last chapter, you might find it useful to see all the ducks lined up in a row; to have a summary of everything you have read so far. First; in most markets, there is an increased degree of volatility, uncertainty, complexity, and ambiguity. And Darwinism applies not only to organisms, but also to organizations: adaptivity (or adaptability) is necessary in order to survive. It is about responding with speed and nimbleness, about being responsive. Many organizations are hindered by their traditional hierarchical structures, lack of internal collaboration, and a tendency to stick to fixed patterns of behavior. But also, because there is such a fear of failure and a too-heavy focus on predictable results, not enough experimentation is done.

Agile management offers the solution: an approach based on the empirical cycle of the scientific method. This has been used within organizations for over a hundred years, visible as the Toyota Production System, agile development, and the Lean Startup.

Agile management is based on eight principles. Creating value for internal and external customers has the highest priority, and that requires a deep understanding of their wants, needs, and behavior. Forming multidisciplinary teams around customers and their behavior is another important factor in this. Empowerment and facilitation are important, in order to optimally motivate these teams to perform. Leadership must find a good balance between teams enjoying autonomy, while being effectively aligned with each other. Teams should work physically in their own spaces, and communication within and between teams should, as much as possible, be face-to-face and visual. Learning through experimentation is paramount to this overall process. This is done in small "projects" with short iterations, thereby achieving maximum speed and flexibility. Finally, teams and team members should be fully transparent in their operations and activities in order to ensure accountability and make continuous improvement possible. This way of working has a number of fixed roles, such as the *product owner*, *agile coach* and—at larger organizations—an *agile manager*.

Within agile management, the *Think–Do–Learn* process is central. This is a continuously repeating cycle built upon short iterations. The cycle focuses on continuously improving performance for your internal or external customers. The *Think* stage is all about setting a flexible schedule based on priorities: what improvements will make the most impact in proportion to the effort? If you're an agile management first-timer, that to-do list of improvements stems from internal analysis of value streams or processes, or from the *customer journey* of your customers. Thereafter, the to-do list comes primarily from the insights gleaned from previous iterations. These insights are made more accurate and effective by using hypotheses and metrics.

The *Do* stage is where you actually get started. Here you build more and more of your products, services, and customer experiences. You get to use the 80/20 rule by working with *Minimum Viable Products*. In each iteration, you deliver something that really works, which can then be offered to your customers to test whether this meets their needs.

The results of those tests you evaluate in the *Learn* phase, in which you use your hypotheses and the information gained from *voice of the customer* sources. Based on your analysis, you can now determine whether your results can become your new default approach, whether you need to start looking for a better alternative, or that you basically have to ditch everything and start anew. Additionally, you can also evaluate at the meta-level to see where improvement opportunities lie in the team's methods.

Briefly, this is what agile management is all about. It lets you transform your organization, making it fast, smart, and nimble. But which approach should you choose for a successful implementation? Here are the Do's and Don'ts.

14.2   Ensuring Successful Transformation

The art of change management has been covered by many good books. Therefore, rather than go into it in-depth, we'll take a look at just a few of the most-important aspects.

No Blueprint

Perhaps you are now looking at the contents of this book as if they are the components of a model kit called agile management. And maybe you now feel ready to glue all the parts of the kit together. Unfortunately, however, there are no standard building instructions you can follow. The way **you** implement agile management depends on the specific circumstances in **your** organization. The form in which agile management is applied varies widely, from organization to organization, and there really is no such thing as the ideal theoretical model. As the old saying goes, many roads lead to Rome. So you will have to use your common sense to determine what does and does not fit your organization. Think of it as a kind of *Barbapapa,* an adaptable set of eight agile principles that can be translated to the needs and situation of your organization.

During the implementation, you will encounter challenges: part-time workers, home workers, flexible workplaces, physical limitations in your office space, several office locations, long-term sick, managers, and employees who can't or don't want to participate and so on. The practice is naturally unruly. Focus, then, on what *can* be done and strive for the maximum possible. Better to do something small, very well, than something big badly. Whatever you do, work with fixed, short *iterations*, *time-box* all your discussions and meetings, and make minor improvements based on *backlogs* and agreed roles. That is the basic approach, the minimum. Keep in mind that impossibilities are sometimes illusory: something might seem impossible because the people involved are looking through a lens of limiting beliefs. Be prepared for it to get worse before it gets better, but research shows you can trust that it will improve rapidly (if you're doubtful, try Googling "Satir curve").[69]

So be proactive and use the resources in this book to arrive at a creative solution, the way the A-Team always managed to save the direst situation. Then, like Hannibal Smith, you can say to your A(gile) team, "I love it when a plan comes together."

Changing, Out of Urgency, and Ambition

For many people in your organization, transitioning to agile management will entail uncertainty. Some people do not like change, some cannot change—or both. You take them out of their comfort zone and that produces tension. It helps to appeal to a sense of urgency and ambition in these individuals, as you can see in Figure 14.1. Try to make the problems that arise explicit, and specific to the individual concerned, and then show them what it can bring them; answer their "What's in it for me?" questions.

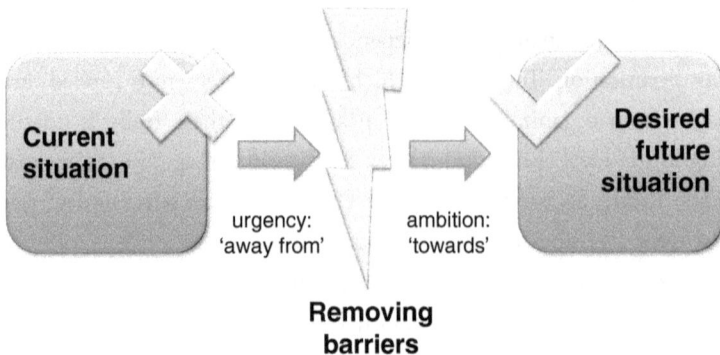

Figure 14.1 *Make the urgency and ambition of the change clear*

The sense of *urgency* is, therefore, the pain the organization feels in the current situation, such as increased competition, declining profit, and customer dissatisfaction. Often, this means that it is the organization's fixed strategies that threaten its future existence. For *ambition* is really all about inspiration. This may concern a major strategic opportunity, within one or more quadrants of the Ansoff matrix (see section 9.1). Or it might be about a visionary, energizing purpose in the future, also known as a BHAG (*Big Hairy Audacious Goal*)[1] or the "*Why.*"[2] Here are a few quick examples: Henry Ford wanted to make the car available to everyone; Facebook is committed to an open and connected world; Google wants to organize the world's information to make it universally accessible and useful; SpaceX wants to make it possible to visit Mars and even live there. Now, of course, comes the "million-dollar question": do you know what you want to achieve with your own organization?

If your urgency and ambition are clear and obvious, you can then explain exactly what is holding the organization back (see section 7.4). And, naturally enough, what the solution is: transformation into an agile management organization. Once again we look to visualization for clarity, for instance with a so-called *transformation storymap*. That is a drawing or animation of the journey from the current situation to the desired situation and the problems to be overcome en route.

Agile-Change to an Agile Organization

Flexibility is essential and applies to both the content and the form, the way you go about it. You could call it an agile implementation of agile management. In other words, apply the principles of agile management also to your approach to change; practice what you preach. Create a multidisciplinary *change team*, your "guiding coalition,"[72] which also will function via *sprints* and *backlogs*. Communicate, within and outside this team, as much as possible face-to-face and visually. Immerse yourself in the *personas* of your "change target groups" and their *customer journeys* within your change process. Take small steps that bring them something tangible. Measure the impact and evaluate the result, and so learn how to perform the next step even better. And keep Willy Brandt's wisdom in mind: "Small steps are better than no steps."

It is, therefore, sensible to start small, with an experiment, a pilot; for instance, by highlighting a specific, discrete customer process, one that is clear and easily defined, and then set a small agile team to work on it. Don't start half-hearted, by splitting their time between the new agile project and their current responsibilities. They need to go at it full-on, preferably in a designated *war room*. There's no place for doubt and faint hearts. You should not change your whole organization at once, but where you choose to do it, you have to do it completely. On a small scale, you'll gain experience and achieve rapid, repeated success that you can use as evidence to convince the rest of the people in your organization that this is an attractive option for them too. Then you can involve other teams step-by-step. As *agile's* reputation grows within the organization, it will spread like a virus, until you achieve "critical mass" and its full speed ahead.

A "Must-Win Battle"

Dwight Eisenhower once sighed: "I have two kinds of problems, the urgent and the important. The urgent are not important, and the important are not urgent." In order to prioritize his tasks, he developed the—now famous—*urgent/ important matrix* and tried to focus on issues that were important, but were not urgent. So you can move forward in a structured way. That can be achieved, for example by positioning the transformation in your change communication as a *must-win battle*.[73] This is a fight that, in not more than the next two years, your organization must absolutely win to achieve its strategic goals. In other words, a concrete and realizable initiative that makes a significant difference to your customers and gives everyone involved a lot of energy—and so merits and receives all the attention and resources of the organization.

It demands that you create and maintain momentum. To sustain the change, during transformation, you need to constantly communicate about urgency and ambition, about the obstacles and solutions, the "heroes" in your organization and their enormous commitment and effort. And unequivocally celebrate your successes. Given it will deliver favorable ROI, a smart step is to make costs and revenues transparent. The key messages need to be communicated daily, via all relevant channels, to your target change-population. And do not only transmit, but also seek dialogue: in meetings, workshops, demos, company events, and other gatherings, and during walk-in advice sessions and spontaneous conversations. Encourage employees to blog and participate in discussions on your intranet forum. Visits to companies which have successfully become "agile" are very useful, as is creating a company "library" of books, films, and articles about agile management.

Securing Each Step Forward

If you have created urgency and ambition, have formed a guiding coalition, communicated about momentum and, with small steps, have extended the agile management approach, it is important now to secure this position. Think of it as a rock climber who, as he gets higher, secures his rope to an anchor point on the cliff. You thus, ensure that employees cannot fall back into their old behaviors and that they feel safe in the new situation.

This can be realized in different ways. Firstly, you need to ensure that the leaders in your organization consistently display exemplary behavior ("walk the talk"). They should be the bearers of the new agile management culture and, both explicitly and implicitly, make clear what is desirable and what is not. Secondly, it is useful to get everyone involved trained and certified for their specific role in the agile management process. And, in addition, they should also be coached while at work in the application of what they have learned. Thirdly, you must structure the organization's governance to feed into the agile principles. The necessary tools can be found in Chapter 8: this is about organizing the *Think–Do–Learn* process, working in *sprints,* and holding meetings like the *daily standup, review* and *retrospective,* and also about HRM instruments like the *reviews.* You monitor this by defining KPIs, measuring them, and reporting on them. You can also regularly hold a surprise audit. And, of course, you also have to adapt your organizational structure, as you saw in the ING case.

But be careful that you don't push too hard. This can best be illustrated using Newton's second law: $F = ma$, where F is *force,* m is *mass,* and a is *acceleration.* Put differently, this reads: $a = F/m$. So, if you want to accelerate (a), it is tempting to put in more and more force (F). However, beyond a certain point, working harder can be counterproductive to the intended change. It is better to reduce the mass (m) of your organization by introducing a certain "lightness" in its processes, staffing, governance, etc.

14.3   Final Words

You've almost come to the end of this book. Hopefully, it has inspired you to get started with agile management and offers you plenty of tools to do so. Remember that it probably will not go easily in the beginning. So start looking for the *believers* within your organization and, together, start an agile management *movement*. A movement that inspires and enthuses by showing the strengths of agile management and that it really works.

Learn to love failing. Just as in agile management itself, you have to dare to experiment during its implementation, only then can you learn from your successes and failures. Become an entrepreneur who does first, and only later asks for permission (or apologizes).

You may regret what you did, but never what you did *not*.

When was the last time you did something for the first time?

By reading this chapter, you'll have discovered the following:

- *There is no theoretical ideal model for an agile management organization. The point is to apply the eight agile management principles. The specific situation of your organization is unique, so you need to be flexible with its implementation.*

- *To successfully realize the transformation to an agile organization, it's best to work in a multidisciplinary change team of believers. That team should frequently communicate the urgency, ambition, and obstacles— and why agile management is the best solution.*

- *Change is best done incrementally. You apply agile management principles to the implementation of agile management. By achieving regular successes, you can extend the approach into the rest of the organization.*

- *To sustain the changes, you must show* leadership *by example and you must invest in training and coaching. Also, you must ensure the governance of your organization matches, supports, and encourages agile management.*

References

1. Collins, J., and Porras, J. (1994). *Built to Last.* William Collins.
2. Sinek, S. (2011). *Start with Why.* London: Portfolio.

Index

OTHER TITLES IN OUR PORTFOLIO AND PROJECT MANAGEMENT COLLECTION

Timothy J. Kloppenborg, *Editor*

- *Improving Executive Sponsorship of Projects: A Holistic Approach* by Dawne Chandler and Payson Hall
- *Co-Create: Harnessing the Human Element in Project Management* by Steve Martin
- *Project Management for Archaeology* by Rodrigo Vilanova, Timothy J. Kloppenborg, and Kathryn N. Wells
- *Financing and Managing Projects, Volume I: A Guide for Executives and Professionals* by Nand Dhameja, Vijay Aggarwal, and Ashok Panjwani
- *Financing and Managing Projects, Volume II: A Guide for Executives and Professionals* by Nand Dhameja, Vijay Aggarwal, and Ashok Panjwani

Announcing the Business Expert Press Digital Library

Concise e-books business students need for classroom and research

This book can also be purchased in an e-book collection by your library as

- a one-time purchase,
- that is owned forever,
- allows for simultaneous readers,
- has no restrictions on printing, and
- can be downloaded as PDFs from within the library community.

Our digital library collections are a great solution to beat the rising cost of textbooks. E-books can be loaded into their course management systems or onto students' e-book readers.
The **Business Expert Press** digital libraries are very affordable, with no obligation to buy in future years. For more information, please visit **www.businessexpertpress.com/librarians**. To set up a trial in the United States, please email **sales@businessexpertpress.com**.